NIGHTS OF OLD: BIBLE STORIES OF GOD AT WORK

AND BONUS BOOK

TURNING THE WORLD UPSIDE DOWN:

SEVEN REVOLUTIONARY CHRISTIAN IDEAS

BY BRIAN JOHNSTON

ISBN: 978-1-911433-15-6

HAYES PRESS CHRISTIAN RESOURCES

The Barn, Flaxlands

Royal Wootton Bassett

Swindon, SN4 8DY

United Kingdom

www.hayespress.org

If you enjoyed reading this book and/or others in the series, we would really appreciate it if you could just take a couple of minutes to leave a brief review where you downloaded this book.

As a thank-you for downloading this book, please help yourself to a free download of "Healthy Churches – God's Bible Blueprint For Growth" by Brian Johnston in the Search For Truth Series:

Amazon.com: http://amzn.to/1FuoN5l

Amazon.co.uk: http://amzn.to/1HTSize

TABLE OF CONTENTS

CHAPTER ONE: THE NIGHT ANGELS
CLIMBED A LADDER

Imagine a lonely stretch of desert with bare wastes of sand and occasional tufts of grass. As the sun goes down, it sets on a weary traveller. If he's dragging his feet through tiredness, chances are he's also throwing the occasional glance over his shoulder - as if to see if anyone is following him.

Why? Well, here's a man with sin on his conscience, for he's cheated his old father and defrauded his brother out of a blessing and now he's on the run. Sin always drives us out. It drove our first parents out of the Garden of Eden. Jacob, the solitary traveller, stopped for the night, thinking he'd put enough distance between himself and home for one day. He found a stone to use as a pillow, and, lying down he sank into sleep. But as he slept:

"He had a dream in which he saw a stairway resting on the earth, with its top reaching to heaven, and the angels of God were ascending and descending on it. There above it stood the LORD, and he said: "I am the LORD, the God of your father Abraham and the God of Isaac. I will give you and your descendants the land on which you are lying...I am with you and will watch over you wherever you go, and I will bring you back to this land. I will not leave you until I have done what I have promised you." When Jacob awoke from his sleep, he thought, "Surely the LORD is in this place, and I was not aware of it." He was afraid and said, "How awesome is this place! This is none other than the house of God; this is the gate of heaven."

Early the next morning Jacob took the stone he had placed under his head and set it up as a pillar and poured oil on top of it. He called that place Bethel. "Then Jacob made a vow, saying, "If God will be with me and will watch over me on this journey I am taking and will give me food to eat and clothes to wear so that I return safely to my father's house, then the LORD will be my God and this stone that I have set up as a pillar will be God's house, and of all that you give me I will give you a tenth" (Genesis 28:12-22 NIV).

Was that the first recorded vow by any human in all history? Jacob says that if God would be with him and keep him safe and bring him back to his father's house in peace, then he'd honour the Lord as his God with any wealth entrusted to him. How could Jacob ever forget the night he'd dreamed this dream: the night when God had made his presence known to him in this place? Jacob marked the place out by turning his stone pillow into a pillar. Surely he must have intended to revisit this place where God had made his presence known to him in this special way by night.

Then he was off eastward again. Down in Mesopotamia, in the employ of his mother's brother, Jacob prospered, accumulating not only a family but numerous flocks and herds. He'd become rich and successful. He'd gained so much, but I wonder if he'd lost the vision of heavenly things? Then, one day, in the midst of his prosperity God spoke to him in Mesopotamia and told him to go back to his own country, making a special point of reminding him that he was the God of Bethel, the place where he had set up his pillow for a pillar and vowed his vow (Genesis 31:13). Jacob then set out for his native land. On the homeward journey, he was once again overcome with fear - not so much the fear of what he was running away from this time – but even more afraid of what he was heading towards.

After all, he'd heard that Esau, the brother he'd cheated, was coming to meet him with four hundred men! This homeward journey was to be another journey punctuated by a strange experience at night. For: "That night...a man wrestled with him till daybreak. When the man saw that he could not overpower him, he touched the socket of Jacob's hip so that his hip was wrenched as he wrestled with the man...the man asked him, "What is your name?" "Jacob," he answered. Then the man said, "Your name will no longer be Jacob, but Israel, because you have struggled with God..." (Genesis 32:22-28 NIV).

Maybe this night-time adventure was intended to give Jacob food for thought - all through his life he seemed to have been struggling to get for himself the blessings which God had promised to give him anyway. It's also true for us that the blessings of the Christian life are found when we let go of our own efforts and lay hold on God alone. Maybe you're struggling with the issue of handing your life over to Christ? Perhaps you're wrestling with the demands of discipleship and the claims of Christ? Then God's word to you is just to yield to him – God made the point more forcibly with Jacob by crippling his natural strength and vigour.

When Jacob got back to his own country, he was surely now a man who relied more on God and not his own strength in fighting for himself. He made his peace with Esau, his brother, and then turned to the south and settled down in a place called Shechem. But, we read that during all that time there were those in his household who must have been practising idolatry. The years passed. If his conscience hurt him about the idols in his household, perhaps he excused himself by saying, "Times are different now". It'd been many years since the time God had appeared to Jacob at Bethel and since he'd made his vow. Then one day:

"God said to Jacob, "Go up to Bethel and settle there, and build an altar there to God, who appeared to you when you were fleeing from your brother Esau." So Jacob said to his household and to all who were with him, "Get rid of the foreign gods you have with you, and purify yourselves...Then come, let us go up to Bethel, where I will build an altar to God, who answered me in the day of my distress and who has been with me wherever I have gone" (Genesis 35:1-3 NIV).

I wonder if Jacob had said to himself. "Bethel, that's where I dreamt about the angels! That's where I experienced the presence of God! Bethel, that's where I made my vow!" It seems clear that Jacob knew he was now a long way from Bethel, not only in geographical location but also in spirit. His mind seems to have turned immediately to those shameful idols. How could he go to Bethel? He knew that idols and Bethel had nothing in common. But this was God's gracious call to go back. We can only imagine Jacob's thoughts and recollections as his mind raced back through the years and he saw himself again as a lonely frightened younger man fleeing from the anger of his brother, Esau. Was it hard for him to find the place he'd marked out, where he'd dreamt that night long ago? There are some places you never forget. So Jacob worshipped God at Bethel, and God appeared to him again. Did Jacob think to himself: 'I always intended to get back here - I don't know why it's taken me so long!'

Maybe it makes you think of some who've wandered away from close friendship with God, from some conviction or vision of heavenly things, perhaps even a vow or commitment they made with themselves and with God. Their spiritual interest has been submerged – perhaps by worldly pleasures – but it's still there below the surface of their life, like the fabled submerged city of Atlantis. Did you know England has its very own Atlantis? It's a village called Mardale. Long ago it became submerged under the surface of Haweswater reservoir. The year 2003 was one of the driest years on record in the United Kingdom, during which the long-lost walls from the submerged village of Mardale reappeared and even began to dry off in the autumn sun. Some parts of the outskirts of the village poked above the waters of the reservoir for the first time since the drought year of 1995.

Our spiritual life with God can become like that – it can get submerged, covered with the temporary currents of this world. But deep down the interest is still there, and it shows itself now and again. For some people, spiritual interest is rekindled at a mother's deathbed, in some moment of awakening conscience, in the hour of distress or danger, or deliverance from illness or death. It's relatively easy to vow and promise to serve the Lord – but sadly just as easy to walk away from it. There are plenty of people today who would hardly be recognized as the same people their friends saw ten, twenty, or thirty years ago. The ladder and the angels have faded away from view. The world will never tell you to go back, for the world's business is to keep you as far as possible from Bethel and to drown out any spiritual interest. No, if you're going to get back to God, God must first of all speak to you. But perhaps today he is.

Perhaps through this book God's asking you to come back to himself, and to live up to your earlier commitments – to serve him once again at your highest level of commitment. Are you, like Jacob, willing to put away all that hinders, and get right back there?

CHAPTER TWO: THE NIGHT WHEN DEATH STALKED THE LAND

Some of the greatest events in the history of the Bible took place at night. In this chapter we'll look at one I'm calling "the night when death stalked the land." It was a night that would open a new chapter in God's dealings with the world. Its setting is the ancient land of Egypt.

At the time in history when this story is set, terrible plagues have recently troubled the land of Egypt - hailstones have beaten down its harvests; frogs have come out from its waters into its houses; diseases have smitten its cattle and its inhabitants; blood has reddened its water supply; locusts have clouded out the sun; there has also been a thick darkness of a kind that could be felt. Why has all this happened? Pharaoh, the king of all Egypt, has been refusing to release his Israelite slaves. The God of the Israelites has been behind those plagues. Now, once again – but for the last time – Pharaoh's just broken his promise to let the Israelites go free. He's ordered Moses, the leader of the Israelite slaves to get out of his palace. But the same Moses now has an audience with someone infinitely greater than the Pharaoh of Egypt. The Bible next records the words of the Lord God to Moses:

"Now the LORD said to Moses, "I will bring one more plague on Pharaoh and on Egypt. After that, he will let you go from here, and when he does, he will drive you out completely..."This is what the LORD says: 'About midnight I will go throughout Egypt. Every firstborn son in Egypt will die, from the firstborn son of Pharaoh, who sits on the throne, to the firstborn son of the slave girl, who is at her hand mill, and all the firstborn of the cattle as well. There will be loud wailing throughout Egypt - worse than there has ever been or ever will be again...Tell the whole community of Israel that on the tenth day of this month each man is to take a lamb for his family, one for each household. The animals you choose must be year-old males without defect, and you may take them from the sheep or the goats. Take care of them until the fourteenth day of the month, when all the people of the community of Israel must slaughter them at twilight. Then they are to take some of the blood and put it on the sides and tops of the door-frames of the houses where they eat the lambs...

"On that same night I will pass through Egypt and strike down every firstborn—both men and animals - and I will bring judgment on all the gods of Egypt. I am the LORD. The blood will be a sign for you on the houses where you are; and when I see the blood, I will pass over you. No destructive plague will touch you when I strike Egypt...At midnight the LORD struck down all the firstborn in Egypt, from the firstborn of Pharaoh, who sat on the throne, to the firstborn of the prisoner, who was in the dungeon, and the firstborn of all the livestock as well. Pharaoh and all his officials and all the Egyptians got up during the night, and there was loud wailing in Egypt, for there was not a house without someone dead. During the night Pharaoh summoned Moses and Aaron and said, "Up! Leave my people, you and the Israelites! Go...as you have requested" (Exodus 11:1-12:31 NIV).

Just imagine an Israelite child that night in one of the homes in Egypt. He's asking his dad why the little lamb has got to be killed. "Because God has said so," his father replies. "But dad, it's not fair – it's so innocent! For the past four days I've enjoyed having it as a pet. Why can't we keep it?" "Because," his dad replies slowly, "if I don't sacrifice this lamb, you won't still be alive tomorrow morning."

Fourteen centuries later, when Jesus Christ was on earth, Jews were still commemorating this historic deliverance - as they'd done (at times spasmodically) down through the centuries. God had asked them to remember that night in Egypt when he'd smitten the firstborn males of Egypt, but delivered his people wherever the blood was sprinkled on the door-frames. In God's timetable, arranged in advance, Jesus was set to die at the time of the annual Passover commemoration. That was no coincidence, of course. For Christ bore our sins upon the cross and died for us so that by his death we may live. Why did he, an innocent – a sinless – man have to die? The Bible tells us that if he'd not been sacrificed as the Lamb of God, we'd all face God's judgement upon us as sinners – sinners who deserve the fate described by the Bible as 'the second death' – which is to be removed from a sense of well-being, and from God, for ever and ever.

The meaning of the cross where Jesus died is at the heart of the Gospel, God's Good News for the world. John the Baptist said that Jesus Christ was the Lamb of God, who takes away the sin of the world (John 1:29). Paul said that Christ our Passover is sacrificed for us (1 Corinthians 5:7), and Isaiah added that "he was wounded for our transgressions and bruised for our iniquities and by His stripes we are healed" (Isaiah 53:5). There's power in this glorious Good News when a person realizes and confesses: 'Christ died for me, died as my substitute'. Paul said that it was this truth, that 'Christ died for our sins according to the Scriptures' (1 Corinthians 15:3), that he delivered first of all whenever he preached. Yes, Christ did die for us.

During the last year of the American Civil War, a man paid a visit to the battlefield of Chickamauga, where, on September 19 and 20, in the year of 1863, the army under Rosecrans was almost destroyed and was driven back into Chattanooga by the Confederate army under General Bragg. The battlefield was not then, as it is now, a beautiful place with stately monuments rising among the trees, but at the time when the man visited it, it still bore the scars of battle and was furrowed with recent graves. At one of these freshly-made graves the visitor saw someone on his knees, planting flowers. Walking over toward him, he gently asked, "Is it a son who is buried there?" "No," the man answered, and he went on to explain the reason he was there was to plant flowers at the grave. He'd been drafted into the Confederate army, having no substitute to take his place as custom then allowed. But just before he was due to say good-bye to his wife and family and report to the training camp, a young man came to visit him and said, "You have a wife and a family depending upon you. When you are gone, you cannot support them, but I am unmarried and have no one depending upon me. Let me go in your place."

The offer was accepted and the young man went off in his place to the training camp. At the battle of Chickamauga he was mortally wounded. The news of his death drifted back to the southern home of the man whose place he'd taken. As soon as he could save up enough money he travelled to Chickamauga and, after a search, found the grave of his substitute with its simple marker. The visitor was moved by this story, and later when he passed the grave again, he noticed it was now covered with flowers and on a rough board at the head of the grave were cut these four words: "He died for me." Those four words proclaim the power and the glory of the Christian message - "He - that's Jesus - died for me."

It's said that the German artist, Sternberg, once met a young gypsy girl on the street, and impressed by her charm and beauty, he asked her to go with him to his studio so that he could paint her picture. Once there, she noticed on the studio wall a portrait of Christ on the cross. It was one which Sternberg had not completed. The uneducated girl asked who it was. Told that it was a painting of Jesus Christ on the cross, she said: "He must have been a very wicked man to have been nailed to a cross." The artist said: 'On the contrary, Christ was the best man who ever lived and he died on the cross that others might live." "Did he die for you?" asked the simple and innocent child. That question touched the conscience of the artist (who wasn't a Christian). "Did he die for you?" The question tormented him day and night, reminding him that Christ had died for him. Finally, he came to believe the sacrifice of Christ on the cross had been for him, and so he became a Christian. So that's the question I want to leave with you: "Did he die for you?" - "Did Jesus die for you?"

Let's go back one last time in thought to that night when death stalked the land of Egypt: to that momentous night when we imagined an Israelite child asking his dad why the little lamb had got to be killed. "Because God has said so," his father had replied. Remember the protest? "But dad, it's not fair – the lamb's so innocent! For the past four days I've enjoyed having it as a pet. Why can't we keep it?" "Because," his dad had slowly replied, "if I don't sacrifice this lamb, you won't still be alive tomorrow morning." Have you, by faith, taken your stand behind the protecting blood of Jesus Christ? As Israelite children once took their stand behind blood-stained doors on that night long ago? Are you absolutely sure that God's judgement will not fall on you, but will pass over you too? Please don't head out carelessly into a lost eternity. Turn, and find shelter in the blood of Christ. He did die for you.

CHAPTER THREE: THE NIGHT THE DEAD PREACHER SPOKE AGAIN

The outcome of any battle is fully known with hindsight, of course. Hindsight allows us to see what ought to have been obvious before, but wasn't. Our Search For Truth Mailing Centre used to operate from an address in Bolton, England. Hundreds of men from the town of Bolton became casualties of the Second Battle of Passchendaele during the First World War. Few of them were professional soldiers. Mill workers and shop assistants, clerks and railwaymen, they all left the streets around where the Mailing Centre used to be housed. They left those streets in order to go to fight for their country. Few could have imagined the horrors that awaited them on the blood-soaked Western Front. Many would never return. By early 1917, the Battalions of the Loyal North Lancashire Regiment were ready, and on the morning of October 26, 1917, the two Bolton battalions were occupying front-line trench positions in Belgium, ready to try to capture German positions.

Nothing could have prepared them for the next few hours. Tired, wet, hungry and standing in a line of shell-holes with mud like quicksand which sometimes came up to their waists, they waited. When the whistles blew, they advanced slowly towards the German lines and withering gunfire. Although many were killed by the gunfire, just as many drowned in the mud. The battle was a complete failure, and by evening the remains of the Bolton battalions were withdrawn. Hundreds of Bolton men had trained bravely for three years for that day, only to see their lives and hopes shattered in a few short minutes. Histories of the battle rarely, if ever, mention this sacrifice – the darkest day in Bolton's history during the Great War.

With hindsight, there could've been only one outcome to that pointless and costly battle. But it's the night before another battle that we turn to now - another battle that was also a foregone conclusion, declared to be such before it even began. Not hindsight, but God-given insight declared the result of this battle to be a foregone conclusion. How the verdict came to be communicated was as the result of a man visiting a woman at night. The woman was a witch, and her visitor was no ordinary man either. Far off in the distant valley, lay the camp of the Philistine army. On this side of the mountain is the woman with a 'familiar spirit' who claims to have contact with the dead. Suddenly, as we've said, she receives a visit at her home – which was perhaps, a cave. A tall man accompanied by two other men, all of them in disguise, stand there.

The nervous witch reminds her visitors of the king's command against practising witchcraft – a command carrying the death penalty for any who should invoke the dead. But the tall stranger reassures her, guaranteeing her safety. Then the woman asks, "Whom shall I bring up for you?" Her visitor, who is the disguised king of Israel, Saul, answers, "Bring up Samuel for me." The witch, we imagine, went through her usual ritual, and then to her shock horror, in this case, Samuel really did appear. At once, the woman knew her client was none other than King Saul himself. The king, who apparently at first either didn't see Samuel or if so didn't recognize him, said to her: "Don't be afraid. What do you see?" The woman said, "I see a spirit coming up out of the ground." "What does he look like?" he asked. "An old man wearing a robe is coming up," she said. Then Saul knew it was Samuel, and he bowed down" (1 Samuel 28:13-14 NIV).

The last time Samuel and Saul had met hadn't been a happy occasion. It had been the time when Saul had disobeyed God by not completely destroying the army of the Amalekites. When confronted by Samuel at that time, Saul had replied: "I have sinned. But please honour me...So Samuel went back with Saul...Then Samuel left for Ramah...Until the day Samuel died, he did not go to see Saul again" (1 Samuel 15:30-35 NIV). Saul had never again had another interview with Samuel while he was alive; and now he was trying to interview him after his death. Consulting mediums was, of course, something God has outlawed in the Bible. In fact, God has pronounced himself against it in the strongest possible terms. As a result, Saul himself had banned the practice. This apparently had the effect of driving witches - quite literally - underground.

But Saul is now a desperate man, and deliberately does what he knows to be wrong. He'll stop at nothing. In fact, he feels he's nothing to lose since God won't speak to him. To the prostrate king, Samuel said sternly: "Why have you disturbed me by bringing me up?" "I am in great distress," Saul said. "The Philistines are fighting against me, and God has turned away from me. He no longer answers me, either by prophets or by dreams. So I have called on you to tell me what to do." Samuel said, "Why do you consult me, now that the LORD has turned away from you and become your enemy? The LORD has done what he predicted through me...The LORD will hand over both Israel and you to the Philistines, and tomorrow you and your sons will be with me. The LORD will also hand over the army of Israel to the Philistines" (1 Samuel 28:15-19 NIV).

In the battle played out the next day on the slopes of Mount Gilboa, Israel was indeed defeated - just as Samuel had said - and Saul's army fled. Saul fought on with his usual courage until he was seriously wounded by the Philistine archers. With his three sons dead at his side, Saul, seeing that he had lost his kingdom and his sons and had nothing left to live for, took a sword and fell on it and so committed suicide. In the night before his last stand, Saul hadn't asked to speak to Moses or Joshua or any great hero of the past, but to someone he'd personally known and trusted – Samuel, who'd anointed him as king one bright morning. How promising was the morning of Saul's life, "the spring of the day" as the Bible writer put it so beautifully! Now Saul was bowing out in a dirty sunset.

When Samuel left Saul all those years before, then began the last, terrible chapter of Saul's life. Saul was like a man struggling in a vortex, like one of those heroes of Greek tragedy, battling with fate. What tragedy we find overall in Saul's insane jealousy, suspicious anger, cruelty and remorse! Finally, he ends up consulting a witch, and through her asking for advice from one of the godliest men in the Bible. Such was the chaos of Saul's 'final chapter'. When Saul called upon God in his distress. God didn't answer him. Can we, too, get to a place where God won't answer us? From more Bible evidence than Saul's life alone, we'd have to conclude that the answer to that is 'yes'. Saul made the mistake of thinking that Samuel could help him when God wouldn't. But the night the dead preacher spoke again, Saul finally knew his fate. The Bible speaks of those who: "...although they knew God, they did not glorify Him as God...Professing to be wise, they became fools, Therefore God also gave them up to uncleanness...God gave them up to vile passions...And even as they did not like to retain God in their knowledge, God gave them over to a debased mind, to do those things which are not fitting" (v.21-28 NKJV).

I trust you are not in that category and so I appeal to you by God's grace. Earlier we were thinking about battles that were foregone conclusions, let me mention yet another. The forces of evil on this planet will one day soon be headed up by the Antichrist who opposes all that God stands for. But when the showdown comes with Christ's return to this earth, the battle will be over as soon as it's begun. Paul says: "The secret power of lawlessness is already at work...and then the lawless one will be revealed, whom the Lord Jesus will...destroy by the splendour of his coming" (2 Thessalonians 2:7-8 NIV).

Do you know whose side you're on? Believers on the Lord Jesus will be removed from the earth before that final battle even takes place. But, may I ask again? Are you on the Lord's side, through trusting in Jesus Christ as your personal Saviour? Remembering again those brave soldiers who trained for years for a battle that was over in minutes, let me say this: all life-long we have opportunity to prepare for the moment we meet the Lord, whether as our Saviour or Judge. We won't be kept in suspense then for the outcome. It won't take long. It, too, is a foregone conclusion: "For God did not send his Son into the world to condemn the world, but to save the world through him. Whoever believes in him is not condemned, but whoever does not believe stands condemned already because he has not believed in the name of God's one and only Son" (John 3:17-18 NIV).

CHAPTER FOUR: THE NIGHT WHEN THE WRITING WAS ON THE WALL

The Battle of the Nile was surely one of the most dramatic and conclusive naval battles of all time. It would appear that, in one single night, it changed the course of world history. This was because, by losing the Battle of the Nile, Napoleon was denied an Eastern Empire. How different things might have been if he had won!

Before Napoleon's conquest of Egypt had begun, British spies had discovered his imperial ambitions. Admiral Nelson was then given the crucial task of frustrating them. When he learned of their presence up the coast from Alexandria, he joined battle with the French – at night! It was against the custom of the day to engage in naval battles at night, but this was only the first of the surprises Nelson had in store for the French. The next surprise came when British ships edged between the shore and where the French fleet were moored. The French had imagined they were safe from attack on that side, and had moved all their cannons to face seaward!

Within 20 minutes, the three leading French ships had been silenced. By 8 o'clock the first five ships had surrendered. At the height of the battle, some 2,000 guns roared. Nelson himself was struck by flying debris, and a flap of skin was torn from his head, falling over his one good eye. Temporarily blinded and thinking he was dying, he was led below. But such was the character of the man, he insisted on waiting his turn for medical attention. Then shortly before ten that night, something happened which Nelson insisted on being back on deck to watch.

Napoleon's flagship, The Orient, had been ruthlessly attacked, and by 9 o'clock was seen to be on fire. Buckets of tar and paint had been left lying on deck, and these had caught fire, bringing the likelihood, if not certainty, that the Orient's large stores of gunpowder would detonate. When The Orient did blow up, the sound was heard 32 kilometres away, and the glow could be seen in Alexandria. Destruction on this scale was rare in those days, and so it was a full twenty minutes before the stunned ships had absorbed the horror of the event and were able to resume the fight until dawn.

As a result of that sea-battle at night, the French were trapped in Egypt, unable to resupply themselves or even to leave. Napoleon's dreams of conquering India, like his flagship, were shattered. But it was not the first time that a battle - and an empire - were lost by night. With the help of the Bible, I want to take you back to the last hours of the once great Babylonian empire...

Try to picture the scene with me: night is falling over the great capital of Babylon, with its buildings and towers and the Euphrates river flowing through it. It's here we find the Hanging Gardens, built by Nebuchadnezzar for his bride, who had been homesick on the flat Mesopotamian plains for the mountains of her native land. And this is not just any night, for tonight there's to be a great banquet for Belshazzar and a thousand of his nobles. Imagine a banqueting hall in keeping with the splendour of a world empire. During the banquet, Belshazzar decides to impress his guests: "...he gave orders to bring in the gold and silver goblets that Nebuchadnezzar his father had taken from the temple in Jerusalem, so that the king and his nobles, his wives and his concubines might drink from them. So they brought in the gold goblets that had been taken from the temple of God in Jerusalem, and the king and his nobles, his wives and his concubines drank from them.

As they drank the wine, they praised the gods of gold and silver, of bronze, iron, wood and stone. Suddenly the fingers of a human hand appeared and wrote on the plaster of the wall, near the lampstand in the royal palace. The king watched the hand as it wrote. His face turned pale and he was so frightened that his knees knocked together and his legs gave way...Then all the king's wise men came in, but they could not read the writing or tell the king what it meant. So King Belshazzar became even more terrified and his face grew more pale. His nobles were baffled" (Daniel 5:2-9 NIV).

This act of defiance no doubt greatly amused the king. No doubt the shock tactic had its desired effect on his guests. How daring it was to drink to the health of the heathen gods - the gods of silver, gold, iron, brass, wood, and stone - with the vessels dedicated to the worship of the Most High God! It was as if the challenge was: 'Where is the God of the Jews?'

He was nearer than anyone thought – as suddenly, over against the lamp stand, illuminated clearly by its light, the king saw to his horror the fingers of a man's hand writing on the wall. The king's face turned white and his knees began to knock. It was now his turn to be shocked – big time! Mene, Mene, Tekel, Parsin! Those were the words the fingers wrote on the wall, but no-one could read them. The writing was there, plainly on the wall for all to see, but understanding it was beyond the superstitious wisdom of Babylon. Then the queen remembered the old Hebrew statesman who had served under Nebuchadnezzar. The queen seemingly had not been present at the banquet. It was hardly a suitable place for her after all. But when she heard the news of what had happened, she came and told the king about Daniel, who was able to give interpretations and to solve difficult problems. The king then gave an order that Daniel should be brought in, and he soon made his appearance.

What a contrast between this Hebrew prophet on the one hand, and king Belshazzar and all the party-goers on the other! As Daniel stood there, I imagine his strong God-fearing countenance taking in this scene of revelry that was now frozen in terror! Daniel was polite but candid as he gave to the king the interpretation of the strange writing on the wall: "O king, the Most High God gave your father Nebuchadnezzar sovereignty and greatness and glory and splendour...But when his heart became arrogant and hardened with pride, he was deposed from his royal throne and stripped of his glory..."But you his son, O Belshazzar, have not humbled yourself, though you knew all this. Instead, you have set yourself up against the Lord of heaven. You had the goblets from his temple brought to you, and you and your nobles, your wives and your concubines drank wine from them.

You praised the gods of silver and gold, of bronze, iron, wood and stone, which cannot see or hear or understand. But you did not honour the God who holds in his hand your life and all your ways. Therefore he sent the hand that wrote the inscription. "This is the inscription that was written: MENE, MENE, TEKEL, PARSIN. This is what these words mean: Mene: God has numbered the days of your reign and brought it to an end. Tekel: You have been weighed on the scales and found wanting. Peres [Parsin]: Your kingdom is divided and given to the Medes and Persians." ...That very night Belshazzar, king of the Babylonians, was slain, and Darius the Mede took over the kingdom, at the age of sixty-two" (Daniel 5:18-31 NIV).

Belshazzar is an example of someone who refused to be warned. In his brief, powerful sermon, Daniel reminded the king of the pride of his predecessor, Nebuchadnezzar, and how God had dealt with it. Rather than learning from his mistake, Belshazzar had offended even more than Nebuchadnezzar. He had exalted himself to this very climax of blasphemy by drinking wine out of the cups from the Jerusalem Temple. Neither Belshazzar nor anyone else goes to his doom unwarned. Belshazzar suddenly, on that night, saw a hand writing on the wall. It was writing his judgment, the last chapter in his personal history, as well as his empire's. Nothing could now be changed. Weighed in the balance of the thousand revellers at his banquet that night, Belshazzar was not found wanting. This party had been more than up to standard. His guests had surely been enjoying themselves for, as Jesus said, people 'love the darkness'.

But it's not the judgment of this world that counts, but only God's judgment. And it is in God's balance that we all are weighed. Weighed in that balance, Belshazzar was found wanting. May I ask? What if the hand should now appear and write upon the wall of your room? How would it find you? Would it find you wanting or would it find you trusting? God weighs us all in the balance, in his scales of perfect justice. He's the searcher of every thought, discerner of every secret, and the observer of every act. All of us, weighed in his balance, and searched by his judgment, are most definitely found wanting. But the good news is God has made available for us the possibility of a weight of righteousness that's not our own which can redress the balance. The apostle Paul said that: "God has wiped out the handwriting of requirements (or 'writing of the debt') that was against us, which was contrary to us. And He has taken it out of the way, having nailed it to the cross" (Colossians 2:14 NKJV).

May I ask you, what's your response to that? Have you acknowledged, before a holy God, that as well as the writing on the cross that said; 'Jesus of Nazareth, King of the Jews'; there was other handwriting too - seen only by the eye of faith? Do you believe that the extent to which you've offended God was written there - nailed to the cross of Jesus - and it's as though God looked upon the death of his Son there and then wrote 'Paid in Full' over the 'writing of the debt' - your debt. But have you turned to God yet - and trusted for forgiveness in his Son, Jesus Christ, the only Saviour?

Again, may I ask you to think about this: When the hand begins to write, will it stop with that sentence, "You are weighed in the balances, and found wanting" or will it add, "but found trusting in Christ"?

CHAPTER FIVE: THE NIGHT OF AN AMAZING RESCUE

One of the roughest sea crossings I've ever had was on a ferry sailing from England to the Isle of Man, which lies between England and Ireland. It's a journey I've made many times, and I know the Isle of Man quite well. So I was interested to hear of two fishermen who'd spent the night clinging to the hull of their upturned boat on one of the ferry routes close by the Isle of Man.

In fact, the two men were seen by the crew of a passenger ferry 13 miles off the Isle of Man. After being spotted drifting in the Irish Sea, they were rescued by helicopter. It was an Irish Coastguard helicopter that was alerted and which winched the two men to safety before taking them to hospital in the island's capital. The ferry's captain, described the rescue as a miracle. "They were not exactly on our route...but my second officer was very observant. He told me he had spotted something in the sea. When we came closer I could see it was an upturned boat." How thankful these two men must have been for such a sharp-eyed officer that night!

It's another dramatic rescue by night that I now want to draw to your attention. Darius, the mightiest man on earth can't sleep. Why? Because his conscience has been troubling him. It was what had happened during the day to a man called Daniel that now came back to trouble the king's conscience. We'll let the Bible book of Daniel the prophet give us all the background: "It [had] pleased Darius to appoint 120 satraps to rule throughout the kingdom, with three administrators over them, one of whom was Daniel. The satraps were made accountable to them so that the king might not suffer loss. Now Daniel so distinguished himself among the administrators and the satraps by his exceptional qualities that the king planned to set him over the whole kingdom. At this, the administrators and the satraps tried to find grounds for charges against Daniel in his conduct of government affairs, but they were unable to do so. They could find no corruption in him, because he was trustworthy and neither corrupt nor negligent. Finally these men said, "We will never find any basis for charges against this man Daniel unless it has something to do with the law of his God." So the administrators and the satraps went as a group to the king and said: "O King Darius, live for ever!

The royal administrators, prefects, satraps, advisers and governors have all agreed that the king should issue an edict and enforce the decree that anyone who prays to any god or man during the next thirty days, except to you, O king, shall be thrown into the lions' den. Now, O king, issue the decree and put it in writing so that it cannot be altered - in accordance with the laws of the Medes and Persians, which cannot be repealed." So King Darius put the decree in writing. Now when Daniel learned that the decree had been published, he went home to his upstairs room where the windows opened towards Jerusalem. Three times a day he got down on his knees and prayed, giving thanks to his God, just as he had done before. Then these men went as a group and found Daniel praying and asking God for help. So they went to the king and spoke to him about his royal decree: "Did you not publish a decree that during the next thirty days anyone who prays to any god or man except to you, O king, would be thrown into the lions' den?"

The king answered, "The decree stands - in accordance with the laws of the Medes and Persians, which cannot be repealed." Then they said to the king, "Daniel, who is one of the exiles from

Judah, pays no attention to you, O king, or to the decree you put in writing. He still prays three times a day." When the king heard this, he was greatly distressed; he was determined to rescue Daniel and made every effort until sundown to save him. Then the men went as a group to the king and said to him, "Remember, O king, that according to the law of the Medes and Persians no decree or edict that the king issues can be changed." (Daniel 6:15)

So that was how those jealous princes had made trouble for Daniel. They'd no doubts at all as to what he would do. Neither did Daniel have any doubt of course. At the usual hour he opened his window toward Jerusalem, toward the temple especially, and prayed, and gave thanks before his God, just as he'd always done. The wicked plotters were watching him and with great satisfaction they saw him make those prayers. But others were watching him also. God on His throne was taking notice of Daniel on his knees. When King Darius heard how he'd been trapped and how he'd have to honour his own decree by throwing Daniel into the lions' den – the Daniel, whom he honoured and respected and feared as a righteous man - he was sorry, and more than that, he was afraid. But trapped by his own decree, Darius ordered Daniel to be thrown into the den of lions.

"So the king gave the order, and they brought Daniel and threw him into the lions' den. The king said to Daniel, "May your God, whom you serve continually, rescue you!" A stone was brought and placed over the mouth of the den, and the king sealed it with his own signet ring and with the rings of his nobles, so that Daniel's situation might not be changed. Then the king returned to his palace and spent the night without eating and without any entertainment being brought to him. And he could not sleep. At the first light of dawn, the king got up and hurried to the lions' den.

When he came near the den, he called to Daniel in an anguished voice, "Daniel, servant of the living God, has your God, whom you serve continually, been able to rescue you from the lions?" Daniel answered, "O king, live for ever! My God sent his angel, and he shut the mouths of the lions. They have not hurt me, because I was found innocent in his sight. Nor have I ever done any wrong before you, O king." The king was overjoyed and gave orders to lift Daniel out of the den. And when Daniel was lifted from the den, no wound was found on him, because he had trusted in his God..Then King Darius wrote to all the peoples, nations and men of every language throughout the land: "May you prosper greatly! I issue a decree that in every part of my kingdom people must fear and reverence the God of Daniel. For he is the living God and he endures for ever; his kingdom will not be destroyed, his dominion will never end. He rescues and he saves; he performs signs and wonders in the heavens and on the earth. He has rescued Daniel from the power of the lions" (Daniel 6:16-27 NIV).

God's voice is powerful even when it speaks through human conscience. To think that this King Darius, very likely the most powerful man in the world then, should be troubled in his mind about the fate of Daniel! In the whole of that vast empire, what was one individual? It was within the king's power to order the execution of one of his subjects in any part of the world, and perhaps he'd done that and then sat down to a comfortable banquet and passed the night in peaceful, untroubled sleep.

But on this occasion there was no sleep and no rest and no peace in the heart of Darius. His conscience troubled him because he'd sentenced a righteous man to a cruel and shameful death. This must surely be one of the great triumphs of conscience – the mighty emperor, distressed and uneasy, standing there in the first grey light of the morning at the mouth of the den of lions. Could Daniel possibly have survived? Would his God have been equal to the task of saving him? That was the question he asked aloud when he came near the den. And to his great joy and immense relief, he heard a voice answer from the other side. God had saved Daniel! Although Darius the king had wanted to help Daniel right from the start, the obstacle, of course, had been the fact that Daniel had broken this contrived law - the law that he, the king, had foolishly signed. It was a capital offence to break the law. And in those days the death penalty meant being put into a den with lions. So this had been the king's dilemma. He'd very much wanted to save Daniel, but on the other hand, the law could not be overlooked. There was no way out of this dilemma. So Daniel had been sent to the lions' den where God rescued him.

That story of the king caught in that dilemma seems to me to be an illustration of something deeper. We've all broken God's law – his moral and righteous law imprinted in our nature. The voice of our conscience agrees with the Bible's verdict when it says, all have sinned. And further, the wages of sin is death, the Bible (Romans 3:23) says. For God's own holiness, revealed in his law, demands that all wrongs must be punished. We don't hear much about punishment these days, but deep down we know it's right - if there's to be any real justice that is. And God the Judge of all the earth will do what's right. But at the same time he wants to save us. He hates sin, and yet loves the sinner. It's true that God is love and doesn't want anyone to be punished for ever. But in his holy love he can't overlook sin. So that's why Jesus came and died. In his death he paid the wages of our sin.

The death of Jesus on the cross was necessary to satisfy both God's desire to save us and to satisfy the law's requirements that stemmed from God's own holiness. Now God reveals his love by offering salvation to anyone who will receive it. It can only be received by faith. "For God so loved the world that He gave His one and only Son, that whoever believes in Him shall not perish but have eternal life." This is God's solution to the problem of sin. He calls on us to be sorry for our sins, and turn from them and believe on the Lord Jesus Christ.

CHAPTER SIX: THE NIGHT THE JAILHOUSE ROCKED

To the north rises a ridge of hills; to the south the huge barrier of the Macedonian mountains; between them is a great plain. And on that plain lies the city of Philippi. It's night and, if the city of Philippi lies sleeping, the same can't be said for the prisoners in its jail! For at least two of them are singing! Men have sung songs in prison before, of course, but they've usually been songs of obscenity. This was a different kind of music. Two prisoners in the jailhouse, their feet in the stocks and their backs bleeding from the brutal scourging of the Roman magistrates, were singing praises to God.

Paul and Silas, the two prisoners, would know the songs of the Old Testament – the psalms. I wonder if they sang: "Even though I walk through the valley of the shadow of death, I fear no evil; for You are with me." In any case, as Paul and Silas sang, all the prisoners would hear them singing – and probably responded at first with profanities and ridicule. But the missionaries kept on singing, and I wonder if the hearts of some of the hardened criminals grew soft. But what had happened? Why were those missionaries in prison? Well, it all started when they'd been going to the place of prayer and were: "... met by a slave girl who had a spirit by which she predicted the future. She earned a great deal of money for her owners by fortune-telling. This girl followed Paul...shouting, "These men are servants of the Most High God, who are telling you the way to be saved." She kept this up for many days. Finally, Paul became so troubled that he turned round and said to the spirit, "In the name of Jesus Christ I command you to come out of her!"

At that moment the spirit left her. When the owners of the slave girl realised that their hope of making money was gone, they seized Paul and Silas and dragged them into the market-place to face the authorities. They brought them before the magistrates and said, "These men are Jews, and are throwing our city into an uproar by advocating customs unlawful for us Romans to accept or practise." The crowd joined in the attack against Paul and Silas, and the magistrates ordered them to be stripped and beaten. After they had been severely flogged, they were thrown into prison, and the jailer was commanded to guard them carefully. Upon receiving such orders, he put them in the inner cell and fastened their feet in the stocks. About midnight Paul and Silas were praying and singing hymns to God, and the other prisoners were listening to them.

Suddenly there was such a violent earthquake that the foundations of the prison were shaken. At once all the prison doors flew open, and everybody's chains came loose. The jailer woke up, and when he saw the prison doors open, he drew his sword and was about to kill himself because he thought the prisoners had escaped" (Acts 16:16-27 NIV). So suddenly at midnight there'd been a great earthquake which had shaken the very foundation of the prison, and freed every prisoner. The jailer, awakened out of his sleep and seeing that the prison doors were open, naturally assumed the prisoners had escaped and so drew his sword, intending to kill himself. When prisoners escaped, Rome held the life of the jailer forfeit. This jailer preferred to fall on his own sword rather than wait for the vengeance of Rome. But Paul, seeing his intention, shouted: "Don't harm yourself! We are all here!" The jailer called for lights, rushed in and fell trembling before Paul and Silas. He then

brought them out and asked, "Sirs, what must I do to be saved?"
They replied, "Believe in the Lord Jesus, and you will be saved"
(Acts 16:28-31 NIV).

Saved from what? Not the earthquake, for it was over.
Neither was the jailor asking how he might be saved from the
judgement of Rome, because he now knew the prisoners were
still all there. None of them had escaped. No, it was some danger
other than the earthquake or the judgment of Caesar that this
jailer had in mind. His question had to do with the state of his
soul. He was suddenly concerned about his relationship with
God. In some way there'd been brought home to him that all was
not right between him and God. He now knew he needed
salvation – salvation from the judgement of God, not the
judgement of Caesar. The earthquake might have shaken the
physical building of the jailhouse, but its aftershock shook the
jailor himself to the very core of his being.

I guess it's possible he too might have heard some of Paul and
Silas' singing before he fell asleep, but at any rate he surely knew
why these men – these missionaries - were in his prison. He
realized these men had the answer to his desperate question:
"what must I do to be saved?" Notice what Paul didn't say to this
man. He didn't answer him, "Oh you'll be all right. You've had a
nasty shock. You'll be OK."

Lots of people think that way today, even sincere church-
goers. Something might ruffle them, but basically they think
they'll be OK in the long-run - but this jailer knew he had a soul
and through the Holy Spirit he was now convicted of the fact
that he was a sinner, and that the wages of sin is death (Romans
6:23); and that he needed a saviour. Again, Paul didn't tell this
jailer that he could save himself. He didn't say to him that night,
"Stop any mistreating of your prisoners and let the dramatic
events of this night teach you a lesson". No, in his midnight hour

of need, Paul didn't tell the jailer that he could save himself; but he told him the true and only way to be saved from the judgement which our flawed character and wrong-doing deserves. We're sinners by nature and practice and the only possible answer is: "Believe in the Lord Jesus, and you will be saved."

Paul's answer is still the Bible's only answer. Let's try to see what it means. It seems there are different kinds or levels of faith. We might speak of faith in one another, or faith in the laws of the universe. Still higher is faith in God: that he exists, that he created the world, and that He upholds it and us by his power and providence. Alongside that might be faith in Christ, faith that is, to the extent, at least, that he once lived and died. But even this is not saving faith. What the New Testament means, first of all, when it speaks of faith in Christ, is total reliance on Christ as our only hope of salvation. It's faith in what Christ did for you and me as sinners upon the cross - that by his death we're reconciled to God and have pardon and eternal life as a gift from God.

A young man went out as a missionary to the South Sea islands. John Paton brought to those islands the knowledge of Christ and the Christian way of life. When he was busy with the task of translating the Bible into their language, John Paton couldn't find the equivalent word in their language for the word "faith', and without that word the translation of the Bible would be very difficult to say the least. Day after day he listened to the speech of the islanders, hoping that he might hit upon some expression that would represent what the Bible means by faith. But months passed and the word had still escaped him until one day one of them came into his study and, throwing himself down on a chair, said "It's good to lean my whole weight upon this chair!" The missionary was arrested by that expression, "to lean my whole weight upon." That was the word he'd been searching for! Saving faith in Christ is "leaning your whole weight upon him" for salvation.

When Paul then said to this Philippian jailer, "Believe in the Lord Jesus, and you will be saved," he meant that the jailer was to put his trust fully – full-weight - upon Christ and him crucified. That's the only way of salvation. I hope it's clear to us all that this is not what some have called 'easy-believism'. "Just believe in Jesus and everything will be all right." Paul shares the full message he preached elsewhere – which was 'repentance toward God and faith in our Lord Jesus Christ' (Acts 20:21). Why then was there no mention of repentance in his answer to the jailer? Simply because Paul could see that before him was a man who'd already been stopped in his tracks, shaken to his own foundations, and turned completely about in his thinking – which is what it means to repent! God's grace had already brought him to repentance, had in fact brought him to an end of himself. At that stage what he needed to do was believe.

Repentance and faith is the way of salvation - one that humbles us and exalts God, for we're saved not through what we've done, but by what Christ did for us on the Cross. And it's to lead to a new lifestyle in whoever accepts it. This jailer was saved through his faith in Christ - and as soon as he became a believer, he showed his faith by his works, for in the same night he took Paul and Silas and washed their wounds. Later, he responded to the biblical teaching of the apostle Paul and was baptized in water as a disciple of Christ. Have you declared your faith in that way too?

CHAPTER SEVEN: THE NIGHT OF THE SHIPWRECK

Whenever a train, car or aircraft gets wrecked it's always a terrifying experience. But I wonder if the most terrifying experience of all of those is a shipwreck, partly because of the prolonged strain under which shipwrecked people can suffer before the end comes. The night-time story in this chapter is from the Bible record of a shipwreck, one of the greatest - perhaps the greatest report of a shipwreck ever written. A shipwreck by day is bad enough, but a shipwreck by night must surely be worse. Even when the sea is fairly calm, there's something about a dark night on the ocean that fills many people with dread. But how terrible when there's a storm at night!

It was midnight when a cry of alarm went up on board the ship on which the Apostle Paul was travelling. A storm lasting for a single night is bad enough, but this one had lasted for two whole weeks. You could say they'd been warned. After weathering a previous storm, they'd made it into the harbour of Fair Havens on the island of Crete. But it seemed the crew weren't thrilled with the prospect of spending the entire winter there. Perhaps, there wasn't enough to amuse the sailors. So there had been talk of setting sail again. When he heard this, Paul had warned them that the voyage would be full of danger. But the warning of the first storm, and this warning sounded by the apostle, were both set aside. The vote was they should proceed a little further to a better harbour at Phoenix.

Luke, the Gospel writer, tells us in his other Bible book, the book of Acts, what happened next: "When a gentle south wind began to blow, they thought they had obtained what they wanted; so they weighed anchor and sailed along the shore of Crete. Before very long, a wind of hurricane force, called the "north-easter", swept down from the island" (Acts 27:13-14). It seems that they'd scarcely cleared the headlands at Fair Havens when the next storm broke! All they could do was throw the cargo overboard, and let the hurricane drive the ship along. They'd been 'tempted' out of harbour by the gentle south wind but now, just as they'd been warned, it had all gone wrong.

Day after day, the ship was driven on. Huddled on deck, drenched with the waves and cut by the winds, 276 persons on board now waited for what may have seemed to many of them like certain death. Luke, who was, of course, travelling with them, being the Apostle Paul's companion and personal physician, records – again in Acts 27: "On the fourteenth night we were still being driven across the Adriatic Sea, when about midnight the sailors sensed they were approaching land. They took soundings and found that the water was one hundred and twenty feet deep. A short time later they took soundings again and found it was ninety feet deep" (Acts 27:27-28 NIV).

Remember, they'd already passed through one severe storm before this storm broke over them, and only with the greatest difficulty had been able to take refuge in the port of Fair Havens. That ought to have warned them that the season of year was no longer suitable for travelling by sea. In addition to that, just as they were planning to set sail again, Paul had warned them that the voyage would be full of danger. But the longing for greater comfort – with some pleasure thrown in perhaps - deceived them into disregarding these warnings. So, they had set sail on their disastrous voyage, which now was coming to an end on the rocky coast of Malta.

Luke continues with his record of events as they unfold in the dramatic 27th chapter of Acts: "Fearing that we would be dashed against the rocks, they dropped four anchors from the stern and prayed for daylight" (Acts 27:29 NIV). Well, that was it, everything now depended on those four anchors. And for our voyage across life's treacherous sea, I believe God has given us four anchors: the witness of creation; the witness of conscience; the witness and voice of the communication of God's Word, the Bible; and the witness of the life of Christ, and his death and resurrection. Remember them as four 'C's: Creation, Conscience, Communication and Christ – four anchors for our soul against the atheistic and godless currents of today.

But back again on board with Paul, all through the night the 276 passengers waited and prayed for the dawn. During which time...Paul said to the centurion and the soldiers, "For the last fourteen days you have been in constant suspense and have gone without food - you haven't eaten anything. Now I urge you to take some food. You need it to survive. Not one of you will lose a single hair from his head" (Acts 27:31-36 NIV).

Dawn finally broke. In front of them they could see cliffs with the sea breaking against them. St. Paul's Bay, they call it now, on the coast of Malta. There on an island today stands a statue of Paul. But back to the morning after - once again, we'll let Luke, the eyewitness, take up the dramatic story: "When daylight came, they did not recognise the land, but they saw a bay with a sandy beach, where they decided to run the ship aground if they could. Cutting loose the anchors, they left them in the sea and at the same time untied the ropes that held the rudders. Then they hoisted the foresail to the wind and made for the beach. But the ship struck a sand-bar and ran aground. The bow stuck fast and would not move, and the stern was broken to pieces by the pounding of the surf" (Acts 27:39-41 NIV).

The soldiers wanted to kill the prisoners who were on board, but Paul said that the message of salvation he'd received from God and passed on to them required that all lives should be spared. This time his advice was listened to, and the prisoners were turned loose. We read: "...the centurion...ordered those who could swim to jump overboard first and get to land. The rest were to get there on planks or on pieces of the ship. In this way everyone reached land in safety" (Acts 27:43-44 NIV).

Ten, twenty, forty, fifty, seventy-five, one hundred, one hundred and fifty, two hundred, two hundred and fifty, two hundred and seventy-six! All were safe at last! Every one of them! For all of them had finally obeyed the word of the apostle Paul in the message of salvation which he had received from God. The whole ship's company had escaped death at sea. Not one of them was lost! God had promised that their lives would be spared – and so it happened.

Life, too, has what we might call its storms, but all who respond now to the message of salvation – all who believe in Christ as their own personal Saviour will arrive safely on the heavenly shore. Was there a roll-call that night long ago on Malta's shore? Julius, Roman centurion?" "Present!" "Aristarchus, Christian from Thessalonica?" "Present!" "Master of the ship?" "Present!" "Luke, traveling physician?" "Present!" "Paul, Hebrew prisoner on his way to Rome?" "Present!" Two hundred and seventy-six persons in total! All present, all safe at last on the shore. And when the storms of life are past and God's people arrive at length on the heavenly shore and the Lord Jesus Christ, the Captain of our Salvation calls the roll on heaven's shore – may I ask - will you be there, saved through faith in Christ alone?

CHAPTER EIGHT: A NIGHT TO END ALL NIGHT FOR EVER!

In Bethlehem mothers would have been lulling their babies to sleep. In the courtyards of the inn, the cattle too, I guess, would've been settling down for the night. And in the fields the sheep would also have been lying down while the shepherds perhaps sat around their fires. But, in what was likely to have been the stable of the inn, a virgin mother gave birth and laid her child in a manger. All the plans for the arrival of the Saviour of the world finally materialized on this one night.

This unique event, on this night of nights, had been promised for a long time. Straight after our first parents' disobedience in the Garden of Eden, there was recorded the somewhat obscure, but certain, promise of a Deliverer – one who, it was said, as the seed of the woman would bruise the head of the serpent; that latter being a reference to Satan (Genesis 3:15). To Abraham the further promise was given that through his 'seed' all nations of the earth would be blessed (Genesis 12:3). Then Moses tells the people that a greater law-giver than himself will appear in the future (Deuteronomy 18:5). The psalmist then sang of a great King whose name would endure forever, and who would have the heathen for his inheritance and the uttermost parts of the earth for his possession (Psalm 2:8).

Finally, the prophets declared that someone was coming whose "name shall be called Wonderful Counsellor, mighty God, everlasting Father, Prince of Peace" (Isaiah 9:6). In addition to these general promises, there are also very specific ones. The one who is to come will be from the tribe of Judah, of the kingly line, and Bethlehem will be his birthplace (Micah 5:2). Why didn't Christ come say a hundred years before or after the actual time of his coming? The answer is, the Bible says, that he came in the fullness of the time (Galatians 4:4) - when the time was ripe at the end of all the preparation for his coming. The Jewish law had acted in a way somewhat like a school-teacher to prepare Israel for his coming (Galatians 3:24). The tabernacle and temple sacrifices of the Old Testament had pointed forward in anticipation of the sacrifice of Christ at the cross. Christ came to the Jews first, and the enlightened among them were expecting him and waiting for him – for example, the godly Simeon who was waiting for the consolation of Israel (Luke 2:25).

So, it was not by accident that on this night of all nights the Saviour was born in Bethlehem of Judea rather than in some other more famous place such as Athens or Rome. There was a fullness of preparation, too, in the Gentile world. For the world had failed by its wisdom to come to know God (see Romans 1). A dying, hopeless world was certainly in need of the gospel of life, forgiveness, righteousness and hope. The conquests of Alexander the Great had given the world an almost universal language, ready for those who would soon proclaim the Good News of the Saviour. And the conquests of Rome had crushed the warring, independent nations of the world, so that 'the pax Romana' (Roman peace) held sway when Christ was born.

Otherwise, humanly speaking, Christianity would have been strangled in its cradle. But under the Roman Empire's law and government, and over its highways, the heralds of the Gospel went into the world with a common language to preach Christ. The time had come. God's hour had struck on that night of the Saviour's birth in Bethlehem. What unfolds to us in that night is what the apostle Paul described as "the mystery of godliness: God...manifest in the flesh" (1 Timothy 3:16).

In the gospel accounts by Matthew and Luke we have a historical narration of the facts of how he came. Christianity depends upon the truth of its great facts. It can't be ethically and morally true and at the same time historically false. Without this record of Jesus' birth – without the Bible declaring that this was God in heaven sending his own Son into the world – Christ's life would be the greatest of all riddles. And we rejoice that he came in the way that he did. God not only sent his only Son into the world, but he sent him in a way that forever touches our hearts. The charm of 'the Christmas story' lies in the way Christ came to earth: the star guiding the philosophers from the East; the wondering of the girl from Nazareth at what the angel had told her; the virgin mother arriving at Bethlehem where there was no room for them in 'the inn'; the manger cradle; the lowing cattle; the praise of the angels; the bowing shepherds...

We're not left in any doubt as to the purpose of that wonderful birth that night in Bethlehem. The angel of the Lord said to Joseph that the child to be born was to be named Jesus because "he will save his people from their sins" (Matthew 1:21). The angel told the shepherds that a Saviour was born to them. Later in his writing, the disciple John said that Jesus came to bring light and life into the world.

The apostle Paul, also writing in the Bible (1 Timothy 1:15), said that Jesus had come to save sinners, and Jesus himself, summed it all up by saying that he came to "seek and to save that which was lost" (Luke 19:10). The child that was born on this night of nights was born to die upon the cross for the salvation of all who come to believe in him. It was through his birth and death that he'd come to seek and to save that which was lost. The coming of Christ was all about bringing peace between God and man, the peace of forgiveness - not political peace. But if all of us were to receive that peace, we'd have peace between the nations too.

Mentioning the connection between Christ's coming and peace on earth, reminds me that recently a book of memories has been published to document a strange, but apparently true, happening amid all the carnage of the fighting of the Great War. In the first months of World War I, while the mud was still new to the troops in the trenches, and the killing also was still novel to them, Christmas approached. Some of the soldiers on both sides crossed no-man's-land and met to exchange gifts, sing carols, play games of soccer, and socialize. This so- called Christmas truce lasted in some sectors for several days or even a couple of weeks. It was declared by the soldiers over the Christmas Holiday in 1914. Officers repeatedly (as reported in the book Silent Night: The Story of the World War I Christmas Truce), but unsuccessfully tried to stop this friendly behaviour, for they feared the men wouldn't be able to go back to the business of killing each other afterwards.

The mud of Flanders had covered the German grey and the British khaki alike and given everyone a common uniform. The soldiers who had been trying to kill one another, now extended their hands to each other and spent the morning and afternoon of Christmas Day in brotherly friendship, with singing and the swapping of presents.

Through that brief period on the battlefields of Flanders, when German and British soldiers spontaneously agreed to declare a truce and suspend fighting, we sense how much more horrendous the war must have been for them after they'd clasped hands and focused on their common humanity. But as the light of Christmas Day faded, the men in grey and the men in khaki did go back to their dismal trenches and the killing began again. I wonder, will our thoughts about the Saviour, Christ the Lord, leave us just as quickly? Will we go straight back to our old ways of behaving? Or will the Saviour born on that night of all nights make a real, an eternal difference to us? – a lasting difference that'll more and more be seen in us by others.

With that challenging thought for all of us, we come to an end of this book in which we've looked together at many important nights in the Bible. Some, we've seen, were nights of destiny as when world empires changed hands overnight; others were nights of individual heroic faith, involving the likes of Daniel and Paul. We've concluded our studies with the high point: the greatest night of all – the night when the Saviour came to earth, and was cradled in Bethlehem's manger. But I want to leave you with this amazing thought. He was born at night that we might experience no more night! At the very end of the Bible, we're given a glimpse of what it'll be like for believers in the world to come. One of the many striking features in the description we find there is this: "There will be no more night" (Revelation 22:5 NIV).

Please, don't refuse the invitation of Bethlehem's Saviour for, if you do, you will go out into eternal night. You may remember that it's written of Judas, the betrayer, that he went out...and it was night (John 13:30). Instead, I ask you to follow the Everlasting Light, born that night two thousand years ago, so that for us it'll be a case of 'no more night' for ever and ever.

BONUS BOOK: TURNING THE WORLD UPSIDE DOWN!

BONUS CHAPTER ONE: DEATH IS NOT THE END!

Oxford professor, John Lennox, says he was travelling on the train to London, and there was sitting beside him a man in his late 50s who was reading what was obviously a scientific article. Lennox said: 'I see you're a scientist'. He said, 'That's right, I'm a metallurgist. What are you?' 'I'm a mathematician', Lennox replied. Lennox next took out a New Testament and started to read it and could see after a few moments the other fellow was glancing over to see what book it was that he was reading, so he made it easy for him to see what it was. And after a moment or two he said, 'Excuse me, you're reading the New Testament.' Lennox said, 'That's right' and went on reading. And after 3 minutes he said, 'I don't want to disturb you, but you did say you were a mathematician and now you're reading the New Testament. How is that possible?'

At that point Lennox asked him, 'Have you got any hope?' The metallurgist went white and started to shake and after a moment or two he said, 'I guess we'll all muddle through.' But Lennox didn't let him away with that, and he said, 'You know that's not what my question was - have you got any personal hope?' And he said, 'none whatsoever.' Lennox then said, 'And you ask me why I'm reading the New Testament?'

The New Testament of the Bible, a copy of which was handed over that day, points to a personal hope that extends beyond the grave for those who receive its message. At a time when the apostle Paul was defending Christianity, he said: "...I am on trial for the hope and resurrection of the dead!" (Acts 23:6). So a personal hope that stretches beyond the grave is a major, defining feature of Biblical Christianity. Christianity gives hope. The first of seven uniquely Christian - and totally revolutionary ideas - which this book will explore is that death is not the end, but that we can have "a hope in God...that there will be a resurrection of both the just and the unjust" Acts 24:15.

Christianity is unique in making the bold claim that all dead people will hear the voice of God's Son and exit their tombs in bodily resurrection bound for one of two destinies. In John's Gospel 5:28, Jesus says: "all who are in the tombs will hear His voice, and will come forth". Notice, Jesus plainly says that all will be bodily raised. How better could he prove the authority of his words than by his own bodily resurrection after his sacrificial death on the cross?

Professor Thomas Arnold, former chair of history at Oxford stated, "I have been used for many years to study the histories of other times, and to examine and weigh the evidence of those who have written about them, and I know of no one fact in the history of mankind which is PROVED BY BETTER AND FULLER EVIDENCE of every sort, than the great sign which God has given us that Christ died and rose again from the dead."

As such then, it gives objective, testable, and decisive evidence for the Christian faith. As the Apostle Paul says: "if there is no resurrection of the dead, [then] not even Christ has been raised; and if Christ has not been raised, then...your [Christian] faith also is vain" 1 Corinthians 15:14.

Christians, Jews, and most informed atheists agree that Jesus was crucified and buried. The crucial belief for Christianity is that he was also resurrected — proving he's the Son of God, and the unique way of salvation for all who truly believe in him. As Paul says this is the critical evidence for Christianity and what's exciting is that it's testable as an objective fact of history - and in exactly the same way that any other historical claim can be established as fact. The questions we need to ask are: 'what's the evidence?' and 'which possible explanation best fits the evidence?'

Beginning with the evidence for the empty tomb then, Matthew's Gospel goes on to support the claim of Jesus' resurrection by volunteering the information that the guards who'd been assigned to stand watch over the tomb of Jesus..."came into the city and reported to the chief priests all that had happened. And when they had assembled with the elders and consulted together, they gave a large sum of money to the soldiers, and said, "You are to say, 'His disciples came by night and stole Him away while we were asleep'" Matthew 28:11-13.

So an alternative explanation, that the disciples simply stole Jesus' body, was the first to be put forward by the earliest opponents of Christianity. But I want you to notice that this was in order to explain away the empty tomb. We shouldn't skim over this. The point was conceded at the time - by those hostile to Christianity - that the tomb was standing empty!

Now for the evidence of eyewitnesses: the Gospels report that women were the first eyewitnesses of the empty tomb and the risen Christ - but the testimony of women was not legally accepted in that culture then. So it's unlikely the Gospel writers would use it if they were simply inventing a story. The apostle Paul, also appealed to eyewitness evidence for Jesus' resurrection in order to show that Christianity is true. In the fifteenth chapter of Corinthians, he wrote: "that Christ died for our sins according to the Scriptures, and that He was buried, and that He was raised on the third day according to the Scriptures, and that He appeared to Cephas, then to the twelve. After that He appeared to more than five hundred brethren at one time, most of whom remain until now..." 1 Corinthians 15:3-6.

Why did Paul add that last remark – about most of the eyewitnesses being still alive at that time? This level of detail is evidence of a genuine account. But more than that, surely it was inviting the audience to go and interrogate the eyewitnesses themselves! And the only people we know of who actually questioned early eye-witnesses changed their verdict and became believers - which brings us finally to the evidence of transformed lives.

There are two outstanding examples: James the Lord's half-brother and the rabbi, Saul from Tarsus. Their U-turn from total disbelief and violent hostility is hard to explain if the resurrection never happened. Concerning the others, Mark tells us in his Gospel (Mark 14:50) how at the first, "they all forsook [Jesus], and fled". But something immensely significant must have happened to that small band of frightened and humiliated men, for less than two months later, they went back into Jerusalem to preach boldly, and at the threat of death, that Jesus Christ was alive! Luke records them saying in Acts 4:20: "For we cannot but speak the things which WE HAVE SEEN AND HEARD".

Many of them would go on to lose their lives for sticking to their story – their version of events. Oh, I know some will say that people will die for any weird thing they passionately believe to be true – but that's not what resurrection-deniers ask us to accept. If Christ did not rise from the dead, then his followers invented it all as an enormous hoax – and what we're expected to accept is that these early Christians died for the sake of a lie which they themselves invented. That's not at all likely.

Now, if you're a fair-minded person, I want to set you a challenge. You see, one sceptic (Hume) said we should only accept a miracle has taken place if to disbelieve it would require us to accept something which seems even less likely. So, take the various explanations that are offered as fitting the evidence, for example: the 'body was stolen' theory; the 'witnesses were just hallucinating' theory; the 'Jesus later revived in the cold tomb' theory; as well as the view that Jesus really did rise from the dead: and measure each of them against just these three evidences we've looked at: the empty tomb, the number of eyewitnesses and the suddenly emboldened Christians who started Christianity. And ask yourself: which of these explanations explains more of the evidence more convincingly than any other?

And now let me share this illustration with you. It's especially for those who'd want to rule out anything which is inexplicable in terms of our understanding of natural law. A man one day put £20 British pounds in his bedside drawer. The next day he put another £20 pounds into the same drawer. Then on the third day he counts the money in the drawer and finds it amounts to only £15! How can that be? How is it possible that the laws of arithmetic have been broken? Ah, you say, they've not. The laws of arithmetic have not been broken, but it seems as if the laws of England have been broken - by some thief breaking in and stealing some of the money he'd deposited there. That thief wasn't a prisoner to the laws of arithmetic when he stole the money. And neither was God a prisoner to the laws of nature when he became a glorious intruder into our history!

But not only did Jesus himself come back to life after death, he also promised all who place their trust in him will be able to live forever with him even after their death. This has power to give hope and meaning, a hope and meaning which is not wiped out by death: Christians need never fear death – but can actually look forward to it as a blessing.

BONUS CHAPTER TWO: GOD ONCE LIVED AMONG US!

Leo Tolstoy (the famous author of 'War and Peace' and 'Anna Karenina') once wrote of his personal search for the meaning of life ('A Confession' in 1879). He'd rejected Christianity as a child, and after university, he entered the social world of Moscow and Petersburg. There, drinking heavily, living promiscuously, gambling, and leading a wild life, he became ambitious for money – which he achieved through money from book sales and from an inheritance. Now, having money, he next looked for success, fame and importance.

This he also achieved, for the Encyclopaedia Britannica lists War and Peace as 'one of the 2 or 3 greatest novels in world literature.' But he was still left asking the question: Well fine...so what?" At this point, he became ambitious for his family – that he might give them the best possible life (he had a kind, loving wife and thirteen children). But the other question which brought him to the verge of suicide was: "Is there any meaning in my life which will not be annihilated by the inevitability of death which awaits me?" To try to answer this, he searched in every field of science and philosophy. He saw his contemporaries weren't facing up to the 'first order' questions of life...like where did I come from? Who am I? Where am I going? He eventually found that the peasant people of Russia had the answer - in their Christian faith. The hope for which he'd been searching was found in Jesus Christ! So, Tolstoy did find a meaning that was not annihilated by the inevitability of his impending death – and he could only find it in Christianity.

Jesus Christ is the only religious leader in history who claimed to be God incarnate: God come as man. The claim of Christianity is that God visited this earth in Jesus Christ to show just how much he really cares about human beings. Obviously, this is a radical idea, but is it true? Professor Richard Dawkins says about Jesus Christ: 'It is possible to make a serious case that Jesus never existed.' I put it to you that all that statement shows is that we've all got some kind of bias that goes against our better judgement (see Romans 1:18b). Let me illustrate what I mean. I remember once having an old car which I'd patched up.

When it came time for it to go in for its test of roadworthiness I was really hoping it would get a pass certificate. I was hoping against my better judgement, since the car probably wasn't very safe. I was biased against accepting any view of the test inspector which was in conflict with my own self-interest - and anything that was going to cost me money to have it repaired properly was against my self-interest, or so I thought. In the same way, it's just as easy for us to be biased against accepting a view of God if it seems to conflict with our own self-interest. We may not always want a God who's fair - especially if we're conscious of our own shortcomings. That's just one possible bias we might have against discovering the truth.

Having said that, let's face up to Dawkins' challenge when he says: 'It is possible to make a serious case that Jesus never existed.' Actually, this is nonsense. I'll confine my comments to two points. First of all, the historian Tacitus – no connection with the Bible - wrote in 115 AD of Jesus' existence by recording how Nero in 64 AD put the blame for the fire of Rome onto the hated class of Christians so-named after their founder whom he states suffered the death penalty during the reign of Tiberius at the hands of the then proconsul Pontius Pilate. In fact there's far more documentary evidence for the life of Jesus Christ than there is for Julius Caesar – and you don't hear many people disputing that Caesar was a historical character, do you?

Then there's W.H. Lecky who wrote a history of Europe in which he stated that the impact of the three public years of Jesus' ministry had a more profound impact than all the writings of moralists and philosophers have ever had. Ah, you say, I'm happy to concede that Jesus Christ truly existed, and that he was a good man whose moral teachings have proved beneficial to many, but what if the Jesus of history and the Jesus of faith are two different persons? Well, it's easy to be biased, as we've shown, and it's easy to be cynical: one speaker visiting a school assembly to talk to the children about God asked for questions. One lad near the back of the hall smirked as he asked: 'You ever seen God, mister?' The speaker paused for a moment, then said: 'No, but if I'd been around 2,000 years ago, I could have!'

Former US president, Ronald Reagan, once said – and this touches on the Jesus of history being the Jesus of faith - 'meaning no disrespect to the religious convictions of others, I still can't help wondering how we can explain away what to me is the greatest miracle of all ... A young man whose [supposed] father is a carpenter grows up working in his father's shop. One day he puts down his tools and walks out of his father's shop. He starts preaching on street corners and in the nearby countryside, walking from place to place, preaching all the while, even though he is not an ordained minister. He does this for three years. Then he is arrested, tried and convicted. There is no court of appeal, so he is executed at age 33 along with two common thieves. Those in charge of his execution roll dice to see who gets his clothing - the only possessions he has. His family cannot afford a burial place for him so he is interred in a borrowed tomb. End of story? No, this uneducated, property-less young man who...left no written word has, for 2000 years, had a greater effect on the world than all the rulers, kings, emperors; all the conquerors, generals and admirals, all the scholars, scientists and philosophers who have ever lived - all of them put together. How do we explain that? Unless...he really was who he said he was."

The decision we have to make concerning the identity of the historical Jesus has famously been presented like this. Jesus Christ himself claimed to be the Son of God, and so the only options for us are: that he was either a liar or a lunatic or truly Lord of all. You see, Jesus claimed to be God's Son, which if true simply means that he's, in fact, Lord. But, if it's a false claim, then Jesus cannot be considered to have been even a good man (for they don't make false claims), so, in that case, he must have been either a liar or a lunatic (depending on whether or not he knew the claim he was making was false).

We said there that Jesus Christ claimed to be God. You might object and say "Jesus never actually said the words: 'I am God'." Perhaps that's true, but imagine you're out driving one day and your car breaks down. You call George's Garage. Half an hour later a breakdown truck pulls up in front of you with George's Garage written above the cab. The mechanic's overalls and the bill you have to sign both say the same thing: George's Garage. Very soon the car's fixed, but when you arrive home someone says to you 'but did you ask the bloke – and did he say - he was from George's Garage'? Well, no you hadn't, but everything about the man – especially in those particular circumstances - totally convinced you.

That's like the way in which Jesus effectively claimed to be God. What he did, and everything about him speaks for itself. What he did wasn't done in a corner. The works which were his credentials were very public. People who were not yet his followers said at the time that no one could do the things Jesus did unless he came from God. One, who was his follower, Peter, put it like this: "Jesus of Nazareth, a Man attested by God to you by miracles, wonders, and signs which God did through Him in your midst, as you yourselves also know" (Acts 2:22). That last point is important: Peter could say to a hostile audience "as you yourselves know". Even they couldn't dispute the facts. Whereas legends like that of King Arthur were built up over centuries; Peter was talking to Christ's contemporaries.

Born a Jew, Jesus endorsed fully the commandment: "You shall worship the LORD your God, and Him only shall you serve" (Luke 4:8). But, yet, at times, for example after healing the blind man in John chapter 9, Jesus allowed people to worship him (v.38). Put these two facts together and what else can you make of them, but that Jesus was, in fact, claiming to be God? On another occasion Jesus caused quite a stir by publicly saying to someone: "Your sins are forgiven" (Mark 2:9). The Jewish religious authorities who were within earshot were shocked and they protested; "Who can forgive sins but God alone?" Now if someone sins against my neighbour, it's not appropriate for me to grant forgiveness simply because I'm not the offended party. But the Jews knew from their book of psalms (Psalm 51:4) that all sin is ultimately against God. And so, to them, by claiming to forgive a man's past sins, Jesus was unmistakably claiming to be God.

Jesus came to make God known to us. It's because, in Jesus, God came as man, that we really can come to know God. And you could say the kind of character Jesus displayed - in even loving his enemies, for example - is all that we could ever wish God to be like. His was the most attractive human life ever, the ultimate. Faced with that – and coupled with his astounding claims - we must make a stark choice and say either he was in fact exactly who he claimed to be, or he was bad or mad because he was a deceiver. The Bible emphatically describes him as both our Saviour and our God (Titus 2:13)!

BONUS CHAPTER THREE: THE COSMOS HAD A BEGINNING AND WAS FINE-TUNED

The Bible famously begins by saying, "In the beginning God created the heavens and the earth" (Genesis 1:1), and Christianity affirms that God brought the universe into being from nothing, creating it very precisely to support life (John 1; Colossians 1; Hebrews 1: 11). And science most definitely affirms that this universe is quite ideally designed to support carbon-based human life. Astronomer Sir Fred Hoyle – he who invented the term 'the Big Bang' to describe the popular scientific view of how the universe began - admitted it was as likely to obtain a single protein by chance as it was for a solar system full of blind men standing shoulder to shoulder all to solve the Rubik's Cube puzzle simultaneously. And as if that wasn't enough, he added that the simplest cell arising all by chance was as likely as 'a tornado sweeping through a junk-yard...[and] assembl[ing] a Boeing 747 from the materials therein.'

Well, and as we most likely know, some of science's best-established and most widely applicable laws point to this universe having a beginning. And one Nobel prize-winning researcher (Penzias) says that his research (into cosmology) has caused him to see "evidence of a plan of divine creation." In fact, this is exactly what he's on record as saying: "the best data we have are exactly what I would have predicted, had I had nothing to go on but the five books of Moses, the Psalms, [and] the Bible as a whole" (Browne, 1978). In other words, he's saying: the science data and the Bible agree on the fact that the universe had a beginning – at least that's the view of this Nobel prize-winning research scientist.

You may now be asking, 'so what's radically different about Christianity's message then? After all, seems like science and the Bible agree on the universe having a beginning, and being wonderfully suited to supporting life.' The difference, of course, is all about 'why?' Why is it that it's like this? Why should our universe have had a beginning, and be precisely right for life?

The Discovery Channel TV program called 'How the Universe Works', in one of its episodes entitled 'Big Bang', features commentaries by Professor Lawrence Krauss, and tells us: "Everything in the universe is made from matter created in the first moments of the big bang." The program then asks: "How did nothing become something?" Professor Lawrence Krauss answers: "The laws of physics allow it to happen." Then we're told: "At the instant of creation all the laws of physics began to take shape." But how can the laws of physics allow nothing to become something when these laws we're told were still taking shape then?

There is only one way of getting something from nothing (Latin: 'ex nihilo'), and that is by an act of Creation by a Creator—in fact, by the Almighty Creator God of the Bible. We occasionally hear the comment today that there's such a thing as matter being created out of a so-called 'quantum fluctuation' – this is described as being how, starting from nothing, we got equal amounts of particles and antiparticles – in a way that's just like how 'zero becomes +1 and −1' – two numbers whose sum together is zero. And this is often used to 'explain' how the universe popped into existence. But for this explanation to work, it would require the pre-existence of the laws of quantum physics - which is hardly 'nothing', I'm sure you'll agree.

Whenever something is being created, there's simply got to be something doing the creating. There really is no way around that. To say something, even the universe, simply created itself is nonsense because it would first have to exist in order to create itself! Anything which has a beginning to its existence must have a cause. That seems an obviously true statement to make, but let's make sure, let's test it by running it past a famous sceptic. David Hume (1711 – 1776) was a Scottish philosopher, historian and above all, a noted sceptic. David Hume wrote, "I never asserted so absurd a proposition as that something could arise without a cause." (David Hume, in J.Y.T. Greig, ed., The Letters of David Hume, 2 vols. (New York: Garland, 1983), 1:187.)

So, where have we got to? We've reviewed how a Nobel-prizewinning scientist has confirmed the general opinion in modern science which is that this universe had a beginning. And, added to that, we've heard how a leading sceptic, has conceded that nothing can begin to exist without a cause. Taken together, both of these statements mean that the universe must have had a cause. And yet, atheism tries to tell us that the universe just happened, all by chance - and what's more, scientists have discovered that there are famously six numbers that make the equations which describe our universe work - and the stunning thing is if even a single one of them was just very slightly different then we wouldn't be here! In the words of famous scientist, Stephen Hawking, "The laws of science, as we know them at present, contain many fundamental numbers – the remarkable fact is that the values of these numbers seem to have been very finely adjusted to make possible the development of life."

Scientists who don't believe in God – unlike those who do - struggle to explain scientifically how chance, a pure fluke occurrence, could be so precise in its result. Take, for example, Richard Dawkins who's forced to concede that science has – and

I quote – no 'strongly satisfying' explanation on that precise point, but urges his readers in his best-selling book, The God Delusion (pp.157,158), 'not to give up hope' in 'some kind of multiverse theory'- which is the idea that the so-called 'Big Bang, which he believes started it all off, did so in such a way as to produce infinitely many 'pocket' universes of which our universe is but one.

This part of his book 'The God Delusion' hasn't received a lot of attention, but it's actually in print that this strident voice of atheism appeals to his readers not to give up hope in the discovery of some new scientific theory that'll one day save atheism! Isn't there a hint of desperation there? But through the media, the impression is still usually given that science has somehow disproved God.

But how does this weird idea help Dawkins anyway? Well, it's a notion that builds on the idea that it's rare to throw 3 sixes in a row with a single die, but if instead you have enough people - 216 to be precise – and they're all throwing dice then you would in fact expect to find someone among them who does in fact get 3 sixes in a row. Arguing like that, they say that if there are a trillion trillion parallel universes, you'd expect there to be one – and it turns out to be ours - which is finely-tuned in exactly the way ours is. That's really the best Dawkins' science can do as a way of explaining how we're here at all as we are.

The choice we're faced with, then, is a blind faith in a trillion trillion other universes or rational faith in a single creator God – but notice one way or the other, it's down to faith. But I'd like to ask you which kind of faith is the most reasonable? One which believes that information and powers of scientific reasoning have their source in the mind of a super-intelligent creator God; or, a faith that believes that our ability to reason arose out of random mindless processes – but is somehow still to be trusted!

As we've heard, those who sustain their atheistic belief in the 'mere appearance' of design put forward the idea - totally without evidence - that myriads of so-called parallel universes exist. What they're doing is literally trying to load the dice in their favour. But it remains the case that the extremely delicate complexity of the arrangements necessary for life on this planet are far less well explained by the assumption - or belief - that life is purely the result of an accidental combination of chance events.

This fact is so remarkable that Antony Flew, an academic who promoted atheism for most of his adult life, stated – not long before he died - that the fine-tuned universe arguments had finally undermined his atheism – and by contrast had convinced him to the point where he said, "I am very much impressed [with] the case for Christianity" ('There is a God', by A. Flew). That's an example which shows how this unique and revolutionary idea of Christianity can be a very telling one – and is where the evidence leads us.

The first three ideas which we've shared in this series so far are all summed up in the public address which the Apostle Paul's delivered in Athens: "The God who made the world and everything in it...made from one man every nation of mankind to live on all the face of the earth, having determined allotted periods and the boundaries of their dwelling place, that they should seek God, in the hope that they might feel their way toward him and find him. Yet he is actually not far from each one of us...The times of ignorance God overlooked, but now he commands all people everywhere to repent, because he has fixed a day on which he will judge the world in righteousness by a man whom he has appointed; and of this he has given assurance to all by raising him from the dead" (Acts 17:27-31).

God says "come let us reason together" in Isaiah 1:18 and Jesus Christ, his Son, says "Come to me."

BONUS CHAPTER FOUR: CHRISTIANITY EXPLAINS THE UNIVERSE BETTER THAN ATHEISM DOES!

At Athens, the ancient centre of learning, Paul's reasoned case for Christianity caught the attention of some who belonged to various schools of philosophy. Some of them effectively wrote Paul off as a 'babbler.' The actual word they used literally described Paul as a 'seed-picker.' It seemed to picture someone gathering up seeds in order to scrape together a meal for himself, just as some desperate person today might sift through rubbish bins or garbage cans in order to find enough food to live on. Applied to Paul, they were sneeringly suggesting that here was a poorly educated person who travelled around picking up other people's ideas and feeding on their opinions before trading in them as though they were his own. They couldn't have been more wrong. There are those who give a reasoned case for Christianity today – and they get sneered at too. The sneering may raise a popular cheer, but the intellectual case for Christianity is stronger.

Consider, first, how, if atheism is true, then life is ultimately without purpose. The Nobel prize-winning scientist, Steven Weinberg, an outspoken atheist, writes: 'The more the universe seems comprehensible, the more it also seems pointless. But if there is no solace in the fruits of our research, there is at least some consolation in the research itself ... The effort to understand the universe is one of the very few things that lifts human life a little above the level of farce, and gives it some of the grace of tragedy' (from 'The First Three Minutes'). Weinberg considers life as being ultimately without purpose, but he does talk about how a passion for actually doing science gives life a temporary lift above the level of farce – and he finds a crumb of comfort in that.

On the other hand, a real sense of purpose is to be found in the Bible's proposition that "we [were] ... created in Christ Jesus for good works, which God prepared beforehand so that we would walk in them" (Ephesians 2:10).

Consider also, how, if atheism is true, then life is ultimately without meaning. In an address to the American Academy for the Advancement of Science in 1991, Dr. L.D. Rue encouraged his distinguished audience to cheat on their atheistic worldview if they wanted to be happy. He recommended that they should deceive themselves into believing some kind of 'Noble Lie' which gave them and the universe some meaning. He said: 'The lesson of the past two centuries is that intellectual and moral relativism is profoundly the case.' He explained that this, when taken to extremes, results in a drive by each of us to live only for ourselves without a sense of community.

To avoid the fabric of society being destroyed in this way, Dr. Rue saw only two possible solutions to overcome this logical result of atheism. One was a totalitarian state, where the wishes of individuals were suppressed by the state imposing its own values on all of society (he didn't want that). The alternative was to embrace some form of Noble Lie. A Noble Lie 'is one that deceives us, tricks us, compels us [to go] beyond self-interest, beyond ego, beyond family, nation, [and] race.' Why call it a lie? His answer was because it tells us the universe is infused with value and because it makes a claim to universal truth – things which atheists deny. Rue adds: 'Without such lies, we cannot live.'

On the other hand, Jesus Christ said: 'I am the way, the truth and the life.' What Dr. Rue judged to be missing is in reality to be found in Christ, and in the Noble Truth of Christianity, when Christ's faithful followers live selflessly "for the interests of others" (Philippians 2:4).

Consider also, how, if atheism is true, then life is basically unliveable. The German philosopher Nietsche, who died in the year 1900, made popular the saying: 'God is dead.' People at that time failed to realize - and many still do - the consequences of killing God philosophically by declaring he doesn't exist. That's why Nietsche concluded 'I have come too early. This tremendous event is still on its way' (from 'The Madman'). But 45 years after his death, the time had come, and everyone since then should know the terrible consequences of believing there's no God. The point Nietsche anticipated was this: in a world which believes there's no God, objective right and wrong can't exist, and so all things may be permitted. When Nietsche's fellow-country-man, Hitler, put Nietsche's ideas into practice, the world soon learnt the horrors that follow when we live consistently with the idea that God is dead, and life is senseless. If God doesn't exist, then our world becomes an Auschwitz. This is man without God. It's life without sense.

On the other hand, Jesus claimed: "I came that they may have life, and have it abundantly" (John 10:10).

Consider, finally, how, if atheism is true, then it's not supported by scientific explanation. Atheistic scientists like Richard Dawkins concede that science has no 'strongly satisfying' explanation for why the universe appears to have been fine-tuned with the precise conditions ideally suited to life as we know it, but he urges his readers (The God Delusion, pp.157-158) 'not to give up hope' in 'some kind of multiverse theory' (the totally speculative idea that a trillion trillion parallel universes exist simply to explain the remote chance of this one being as it is). In this unpublicized section, Dawkins appeals to his readers not to give up hope in the discovery of some new scientific theory that will one day save atheism!

On the other hand: "that which is known about God is evident...for God made it evident...for since the creation of the world His invisible attributes...have been clearly seen...through what has been made...[but] they did not honour Him as God...but they became futile in their speculations" (Romans 1:19-21).

I think it's time to have a little bit of history. Leading the siege of Syracuse in 213BC was a Roman general Marcus Claudius Marcellus, whose nickname was "The Sword of Rome." When Marcellus brought his troops and the Roman navy up against the citadel of Syracuse, the Romans encountered frightful war machines they'd never seen before, and far more sophisticated than anything the Romans had invented. One of those war machines was especially astonishing and downright terrifying to the Roman navy: as their ships approached the cliffs outside Syracuse, the sailors looked up and saw huge jaws descending from the sky. These jaws came down, gripped a Roman ship, hoisted that ship a hundred feet or so into the air, and then the jaws released the ship and crew dashing them upon the rocks. The Romans couldn't believe what they were seeing as ropes and metal manipulated by the unheard of technical marvels of pulleys and levers, came down and gripped their ships. However, eventually, the Romans were victorious.

General Marcellus' command was that the engineer who'd developed these new weapons was to be unharmed, when and if he was found. But as a Roman soldier approached the engineer as he was sitting with other prisoners; he found him passing the time by doing mathematical equations in the sand. The man was so absorbed in calculation that he didn't notice it was a Roman soldier. Without taking his eyes off his calculations in the sand he said, "Be careful! Do not disturb my diagrams!" And the Roman soldier killed him on the spot. And thus Archimedes met his death...

Greek by birth, born in 287 BC in Syracuse to Greek parents, educated in Alexandria, Egypt, Archimedes went on to become a remarkable mathematician, an exacting engineer, a brilliant inventor, an master craftsman, a skilful builder, and something of a philosopher. It was Archimedes who, so it is claimed, after having figured out the laws of buoyancy as he was stepping into his bathtub, ran into the streets naked crying out "Eureka! (I've found it!)" Archimedes defined the principle of the lever, and is credited with inventing the compound pulley. He was one of the most brilliant men, not only of the ancient world, but of all time.

You may know the words he spoke to the king of Syracuse on one occasion: "Give me a lever long enough, and a place to stand, and I will move the whole world." A little over two hundred years after Archimedes made that statement a lever was indeed found that was long enough to move the whole world. Revealed in the Gospel of the cross is the power of God to set right a topsy-turvy world. It was the message of the cross, which created the necessary leverage that continues to change the world.

Acts 17:6 reads, "These men who have turned the world upside down..." when referring to Paul and Silas who used that Gospel lever to turn their world upside down. By the way, when the Bible speaks of turning the world upside down, it's really speaking in terms of turning the world right side up. For we live in a topsy-turvy world, a world where all around us the wicked prosper, and the righteous suffer; where sin is often exalted, and virtue mocked; a world in which it's been said that "Beggars ride on horseback while princes walk in rags." Ever since Eden, this world has been the wrong way up. And the message of Christianity is about what God has done, through the cross of Christ, to turn the world the right way up again. That's why this book is show-casing the revolutionary, or counter-cultural, ideas of the Christian message.

BONUS CHAPTER FIVE: SALVATION IS BY GOD'S GRACE, NOT BY OUR OWN WORKS

Through our high opinion of modern achievements, our society deceives us into thinking that we can do anything. Probably nothing did more to promote this illusion than Dale Carnegie's blockbuster book 'How to Win Friends and Influence People.' It was all about how to put the other person in a position where he or she cannot decently say 'no'. From this, optimism spills over to the belief that we can even repair our relationship with God. After all, we've long since learned to split the atom and put a man on the moon.

Just as the pagans long ago believed they could put their gods in a position of not being able to say no to them by means of offering them gifts and sacrifices; nowadays we think we can do the same by our church-going and good deeds. But the sober reality is that we simply can NOT do anything to make ourselves acceptable to God. Regaining God's favour is something that's beyond our power, for the Bible declares "by the works of the Law no flesh will be justified" in God's sight (Galatians 2:16).

The Bible says: "By grace you have been saved through faith; and that not of yourselves, it is the gift of God; not as a result of works, so that no one may boast" (Ephesians 2:8). These verses tell us that our own good works can't save us. This is because, the Bible adds, we're actually dead in God's sight – and that's because of our sins (see Ephesians 2:1). That's why we can't even begin to hope that God will be pleased by our good works and let us into heaven.

Now that's a truly radical idea like the others we've been covering in this series – and this one certainly distinguishes Christianity from all religions. God's not asking us to do anything to merit salvation, he's simply inviting us to receive what he's already done for us in Christ, his son – and full forgiveness will be ours. We do, however, need to be prepared to let God humble us and turn us from our hopeless and helpless position before him.

Please allow me to illustrate how many people think, so that we can realize for ourselves how utterly hopeless belief in our own good deeds is. Let's imagine a dispute between neighbours which comes before a local magistrate. One man is accused of stealing his neighbour's motorbike. This is what he says to the magistrate. 'I am here today to demand justice. I don't want mercy or compassion, I simply want justice. In connection with the theft of the motorbike, I admit that I did it. But there have been many other days when I did not steal his motorbike. I have even done some good things for him on a few occasions. So, on that basis, I demand justice. I demand to be declared innocent and free to go!' What do you think the magistrate will say? Will he be convinced? No, of course not! And neither will God be if we plead that our good works should cancel out our sins.

Let me again try to illustrate why you still might find it hard to accept that salvation from future judgement – forgiveness of sins – isn't something we can influence or contribute to. Vance Packard in his book 'The Hidden Persuaders' – a book I remember being asked to read at school – tells of homemakers' problems with cake mixes in the early days when such mixes first appeared. Cake-mix packages would warn housewives not to add milk but "just add water." Some housewives would add milk anyway, as their own special contribution, and then they'd be disappointed when the cakes or muffins didn't turn out well.

Some cake mixes would also prohibit adding eggs, since eggs and milk had already been added in dry form by the manufacturer.

Obviously, some market research was needed to find out what was happening, why the product was not meeting with success. Women interviewed said: "What sort of cake is it if you just need to add tap water!" So the marketing needed to be changed. The mixes needed to tell the homemaker that she and the mix together could produce the cake. A white cake mix box now proclaimed, "You add fresh eggs." The message was you do have a contribution you can make!

It seems to be in our nature to insist on making our own contribution – especially in spiritual matters. But God in his Word has not changed his recipe for human salvation. The cake-mix recipe might have changed away from 'water alone'; but the unchanging Word of God still says 'faith alone.' It says, "Believe on the Lord Jesus and you will be saved" (Acts 16:31).

Finally, I want to share with you the true story of a pearl fisher. By the time this story takes place, he's an old man (his name was Rambhau) and he'd earned his living on the shore of the Indian Ocean by diving into the water and hopefully returning to the surface with an oyster between his teeth. When opened, the beautiful, shining pearl inside would bring him some money to live on when once it had been sold at the local market.

It was to this same shoreline that a missionary by the name of David Morse came. He spoke earnestly to the old pearl fisher and the other fishermen about the Christian message of forgiveness. He told them how the Bible says everyone who comes to God in repentance, and then receives his Son, Jesus Christ, as their own personal Saviour by faith, is promised forgiveness. The old man, however, was not persuaded by the Christian message. He clung to his own religious ideas. In fact, he told the missionary that the

Christian message seemed too simple a recipe for forgiveness. 'Perhaps I am too proud,' he said, 'but I want to do something to get a place in heaven. I intend to go on a pilgrimage to Delhi for my sins and by doing that I hope to earn God's mercy.'

No matter how often David Morse talked to him, the old diver simply couldn't understand the miracle of God's grace. David Morse tried time and time again to explain to the pearl diver that we can't in any way earn or merit God's grace towards us as sinners - but that we can only accept it as his gift. Nevertheless, even although the fisherman was unpersuaded, the two of them – the missionary and the old pearl diver - became good friends. Then one day, the old fisherman came to see the missionary. He'd come to tell him he was finally leaving to go on his pilgrimage to Delhi. He was being realistic when he told the missionary that he might never return. He was visiting him in order to hand over a little box. 'You're my best friend,' he said 'and I want you to have this.' The missionary opened the box to see a very large pearl.

'I've kept this pearl for years', the diver explained, 'now that I'm leaving for Delhi, perhaps never to return, I want to give it to my best friend, to you. Here you are. That pearl, Sahib (teacher), is perfect,' he explained. The missionary was touched by his kindness, but politely declined. It was much too generous a gesture for the poor old man to make. The pearl diver looked hurt. The missionary tried a compromise. Looking up, he said, 'Well, my friend, let me buy this wonderful pearl, I'll give you $1,000 for it.' The pearl diver shook his head. It's not for sale, it's for you, my friend. 'No,' said David Morse, 'as much as I want the pearl, I cannot accept it. Maybe I'm too proud, but to accept it just like that seems too easy to me. I want to pay or work for it.' 'Sahib,' the diver replied in a severe tone while straightening up, 'this pearl is invaluable, it's priceless. Nobody in this world can pay what this pearl is worth to me. He then began to explain. 'I had a son,' he said, 'who was also a diver.' He was the best pearl diver along the Indian coast. He had the keenest eye, the longest breath. He could dive down to 30 metres. He was the delight of my heart. He always dreamt of finding a pearl better than any that had ever been found. One day he thought he'd found it. But the oyster was nearly inaccessible, deep down and well secured in a rocky crevice.

Finally, he succeeded in getting it out and up to the surface. But he'd stayed under the water for too long. He'd strained his heart. Soon afterwards, sadly, he died.' The old man bowed his head, and for a moment his whole body shook, but he made no sound. 'Now you see, Sahib, why this pearl is invaluable, it's priceless. Nobody in this world can pay what this pearl is worth to me. You do understand, don't you? My only son gave his life to get this pearl. I can't sell it. I can only give it as a present. Just accept it, please, as a proof of our friendship.

Holding back tears, the missionary, replied, 'Don't you see? That is exactly like what I've been telling you about God's gift of salvation. The diver gave the missionary a long, searching look as he ever so slowly began to understand. The missionary continued: 'God is offering you salvation as a free gift, at no charge. It is so great and costly that no man would be able to pay for it. It cost God the life of his only Son to open the door to heaven. Even by pilgrimages of thousands of miles you could never earn God's grace. God's love and deliverance of sinners like you and me – from the punishment which our sins truly deserve - can only be accepted as a gift in faith and thankfulness. God deliberately gave up his only Son to the terrible death of the cross.'

God's light entered the old pearl diver's heart. 'Now I understand,' he said, then he turned around and went away, deep in thought. An hour later he came back and said: 'I don't want to wait any longer, I want to come to God right now, just as I am. I cannot earn God's mercy, the price is simply too great. As a lost person I want to accept this love of God. Though it is beyond my understanding, I want to thank him and his Son Jesus Christ for it.' So, may we, too, understand the radical message of Christianity that acceptance is by grace not works.

BONUS CHAPTER SIX: CHRISTIANITY GIVES A DIGNITY TO HUMAN LIFE THAT NOTHING ELSE CAN MATCH

In the United Kingdom, in December of 2012, the results of a national census (held in 2011) were published which showed that now only one in every three people profess to be 'Christian', while one in four returned an answer of 'no religion.' The actual number of those reporting 'no religion' was 14.1 million, which when compared to 8.5 million in 2001, shows a 67% increase over 10 years in those who profess 'no religion.'

Presumably, some of these people may still have some belief in God despite not aligning themselves with any particular religious organisation. However, many of them will likely be atheists and believe in some form of naturalistic evolution: which is the view that ultimately sees humans as highly evolved pond scum. That doesn't seem to be a very appealing or even a very dignified description of human beings. But the likes of Richard Dawkins would say 'tough, too bad, for that's just the way it is.' Dawkins once said this:

'We are going to die and that makes us the lucky ones. Most people are never going to die because they're never going to be born. The potential people who could've been here in my place, but who will in fact never see the light of day outnumber the sand grains of Sahara. Certainly those unborn ghosts include greater poets than Keats, scientists greater than Newton. We know this because the set of possible people allowed by our DNA so massively outnumbers the set of actual people. In the teeth of these stupefying odds, it is you and I in our ordinariness that are here. We privileged few who won the lottery of birth against all odds, how dare we whine at our inevitable return to that prior state from which the vast majority can never start.' (http://www.youtube.com/watch?v=wfY8tIcJR8Q)

Or, perhaps you prefer the description of human beings as recycled star stuff? Astronomer Alan Dressler has written that every atom in our bodies save hydrogen was once at the centre of a star. We'll allow Neil deGrasse Tyson to explain what he finds appealing in this point of view:

'The Big Bang endowed the universe with hydrogen and helium and not much of anything else. But there are stars, and stars manufacture heavy elements from light elements. They take hydrogen in and fuse the atoms to become helium, and helium fuses to become carbon, and carbon fuses to become silicon and nitrogen, and so on. Thus, elements other than hydrogen and helium have no origin other than [in] the centres of stars. And stars not only manufacture the heavy elements, they also explode them into space. Since life itself thrives on these heavy elements, we owe our very existence to stars.

The very molecules that make up your body, the atoms that construct the molecules are traceable to the crucibles that were once the centres of high mass stars that exploded their chemically enriched guts into the galaxy enriching pristine gas clouds with the chemistry of life. So we're all connected to each other, biologically; to the earth, chemically; and to the rest of the universe, atomically.'

(http://www.youtube.com/watch?v=QADMMmU6ab8)

It seems to me that these are attempts to give some sense of awe and dignity to a hopeless and purposeless existence, but they fail to account for the origin of information. How did the chemical hardware of our cells write its own software? Reducing everything down to chemistry doesn't really get us very far, because if you take the printed page of a book, you can indeed reduce it all down to chemistry – except for the fact that it leaves totally unexplained the fact that the page communicates information through the text – and that happens by the physical ordering of the letters, something quite independent of chemical makeup. If that's true of a single page of a book – and it is, quite indisputably – how much more is it the case that life – with all its DNA information - is more than mere chemistry.

This is where, once again, I want to emphasise the revolutionary nature of the Christian message. How and why is it radical? I would say because it's the only truly coherent worldview. What do we mean by that? First, a 'worldview' is a perspective: a way of interpreting, or making sense of, the world around us. And second, every worldview – and it doesn't matter whether we're talking about atheism, pantheism or polytheism – every single worldview has to be able to answer 4 questions, and these are: Where did we come from? What's the meaning of life? How do we define right from wrong? What happens to us when we die?

You know, these are the four most fundamental questions of life. Every thinking person asks them at some time or other in their life. You'll have noticed, of course, that they boil down to questions of origin, meaning, morality and destiny. And the point is, that in Christ, through the Gospel, we have a coherent set of answers to these four worldview questions: in terms of humans having been created in God's image, to enjoy a relationship with our Creator, who has summarized his moral standards for us most famously in the Ten Commandments, and through the cross of Christ has secured an eternally glorious future for all who believe.

And if I was to select a verse from the Bible to highlight human dignity and contrast sharply with the bleak views presented earlier belonging to those who say there's no God, then I'd choose this one from Psalm 8: It asks, "What is man...?"; and answers, "You have crowned him with glory and honor. You have made him to have dominion over the works of Your hands; you have put all things under his feet." That was God's purpose in creation.

In moving away from the failure of any philosophy which wilfully rejects God's existence – including its failure to invest our humanness with any real sense of dignity – let's now, if we may, view ourselves biblically, and we see that human dignity is something which is derived – it descends from the revealed reality that we're created equally in the image of God. While in certain cases, that image and dignity seems to be more fittingly and prominently displayed than in other cases, nevertheless, the essential dignity of our humanness is an absolute given that doesn't rise and fall within the span of individual human existence – by which I mean it's unaffected by the degree by which our biology is as yet undeveloped or later begins to malfunction.

For even humans who exist in some degree of dependence on others are essentially no less dignified - not, when we reflect on how God by becoming flesh himself in the incarnate Christ dignified even such a state through becoming dependent on human breasts and all the other normal menial duties of care on which every infant depends. In this way, prominent aspects of helplessness are seen not to diminish our essential human dignity which, as we say, is something that's God-given.

In the book 'Finding Your Way', Gary La Ferla tells an amazing story, pieced together from the records of the United States Naval Institute following the Second World War. The USS Astoria had engaged the Japanese during the battle for Savo Island before any other ships of the U.S. navy arrived. During the crucial night of the battle, August 8, the Astoria scored several direct hits on a Japanese vessel, but was itself badly damaged in the process.

At about 0200 hours, Signalman 3rd Class Elgin Staples, was swept overboard by the blast after the Astoria's gun turret exploded. Wounded in both legs by shrapnel and in semi-shock, he was kept afloat in the sea by a narrow lifebelt. At around 0600 hours, Staples was rescued by a passing destroyer and returned to the Astoria, whose captain was attempting to save the cruiser by beaching her. The effort failed, and Staples, still wearing the same lifebelt, found himself back in the water! It was now lunchtime. Picked up again, this time by the USS President Jackson (AP – 37), he was one of 500 survivors of the battle who were evacuated. On board the transport, Staples hugged that lifebelt with gratitude, and studied the small piece of equipment for the first time. He scrutinized every stitch of the lifebelt that'd served him so well. It'd been manufactured by the Firestone Tire and Rubber Company of Akron, Ohio, and it bore a registration number.

Given home leave, Staples told his story and asked his mother, who worked for Firestone, about the purpose of the number on the belt. She replied that the company insisted on personal responsibility, and each checking inspector had their own personal number which they put on the belt when signing it off. Staples remembered everything about the lifebelt, and quoted the number. There was a moment of stunned silence in the room and then his mother spoke: "That was my personal code that I affixed to every item I was responsible for approving." Try to imagine the emotions within the hearts of mother and son. The one whose DNA he bore had also been instrumental in his rescue in the waters that had threatened his life.

If an earthly parent can provide a means of rescue without knowing when and for whom that belt would come into play, how much more can the God of all creation accomplish? His "registration number" is on you, for God, our sovereign creator, originally imprinted his image on his human creation. Then he also took upon himself the personal responsibility for our rescue. He's the one who leaves nothing to chance in bringing all the threads together in our life story. The God who designed us with a dignity – which we've defaced - has now thrown us a lifeline in Jesus Christ – will you stretch out for the purpose you were made for?

BONUS CHAPTER SEVEN: CHRISTIANITY CAN MAKE SENSE OF SUFFERING

I'm reminded of a time when Malcolm Muggeridge, the British journalist and author, had been speaking at All Soul's Church in London, UK. There followed a question and answer time in which the speaker was often called upon to defend his conversion to Christianity. After what had been described as the last question was dealt with, Muggeridge noticed a young boy in a wheelchair trying to say something. He said he would wait and take his question. The boy struggled but no words came out. 'Take your time,' Muggeridge said reassuringly. 'I want to hear what you have to ask...I'll not leave until I hear it.'

Finally, after a real struggle, one often punctuated with agonizing contortions, the boy blurted out, 'You say there's a God who loves us.' Muggeridge agreed. 'Then - why me?' Silence filled the room. The boy was silent. The audience was silent. Muggeridge was silent. Then, he asked, 'If you were able-bodied (fit), would you have come to hear me tonight?' The boy shook his head. Again Muggeridge was silent. Then he added: 'God has asked a hard thing of you, but remember he asked something even harder of Jesus Christ. He died for you. Maybe this was His way of making sure you'd hear of His love and come to put your faith in Him.'

In the answer that Muggeridge gave, with empathy, on that occasion, there are hints of an overall biblical framework which is available for us to use as we communicate the Christian Gospel to hurting people. If shared sensitively, it can help people to at least begin to put suffering in the broader context of God's dealings with a broken world.

And what then is that Bible framework? It's one which would see suffering as a consequence of the separation that exists between God and man. And that this separation has been caused by sin. So we can't blame God for human suffering. The Bible tells us that God created the world in love and that he loves us individually. But if God is good, and on the side of good, why do terrible things happen – like in the mass shootings in Aurora and Connecticut in 2012? What's gone wrong? Well, the Bible's answer is: we did. The London Times leader column said the day after a massacre at an Infant school in Dunblane, Scotland (13 March 1996): 'Christ was born among innocent slaughter and died on the Cross to pay the cost of our terrible freedom - a freedom by which we can do the greatest good or the greatest evil'. You see, the Bible makes it clear that God created us with free will...but then we chose to disobey God and do our own thing. That broke our relationship with our loving Creator. It's this separation between God and ourselves that's the cause of all the suffering that's in the world - and which will finally result in eternal separation from God unless we each personally obey the message of Christianity. For only God has the answer to this problem. And Jesus Christ is God's answer. When Jesus died on the cross, he took on himself the consequence of our disobedience. His death made a way between us and God again. By rising from the dead Jesus conquered the power of death for ever. Now God requires that we each personally repent and receive Jesus, his Son, as our Saviour.

What's more, it's clear that God's concerned about our pain - to the extent that in the person of his son, he came as a man, Jesus Christ, and 'joined us in suffering'. That was the expression used by a Church of Scotland minister when interviewed by a BBC

News reporter on December 21, 1988, when Pan Am Flight 103 exploded in the sky over the Scottish town of Lockerbie. "It was like meteors falling from the sky," one resident there said. Others told how pieces of plane as well as pieces of bodies began landing in fields, in backyards, on fences, and on rooftops. Fuel from the plane was already on fire before it hit the ground; some of it landed on houses, making the houses explode. Twenty-one houses were destroyed with 11 occupants killed. The total death toll was 270, including those on the plane. The reporter savagely turned on the minister and spat out the question: 'Where is your God now?' To which the calm reply was: 'God has joined us in suffering - in the person of his son, he came as a man, Jesus Christ, and joined us in suffering.'

Beyond that, Christ's sacrificial death on the cross for our sins laid the basis for bringing all suffering to an end, but the time for that hasn't arrived yet. And until it does arrive, God uses suffering to work out his higher purposes in our lives - in a way that's not very different from how a surgical procedure involves pain but is directed towards a positive outcome for us. Perhaps that's where the Christian Gospel's perspective on suffering is at its most radical. First of all, God himself, the supreme being, has joined us in suffering. And second, before eliminating it entirely from human experience, he uses it to mature and refine Christian character (Romans 5:3-4; 1 Peter 1:6,7). Becoming a Christian doesn't guarantee freedom from physical suffering on earth while we wait for Jesus to come again and take believers away from suffering to be forever with him. The Bible teaches that God treats as a Father those who are his children by faith and this can also involve suffering for corrective purposes – just as happens in an ordinary human family.

In the town of Baguio, located north of Manila in the mountains of the Philippines, there are a number of gold mines to be found. Small cars on tracks are loaded with rock from within the mountain and emerge from an opening in the hillside. The rock is then crushed, pulverized, and submitted to various chemicals. By this process, minute particles of gold are separated from the useless shale and then submitted to fierce fires in the refining furnace. Later, the molten shining gold is poured into bricks worth tens of thousands of dollars each. Suppose that those stones in the mountains could speak and ask: 'Why do I have to be removed from my place in the hills to be pounded and pulverized, attacked by biting chemicals, and submitted to furnaces?'

A reply might be: 'What use are you buried there beneath the tons of useless debris? You have within you something that's valuable, useful and beautiful. Only through this apparently destructive process can you be separated from the impurities that keep you from the usefulness, beauty and purity that might be yours.' And so, perhaps, we begin to glimpse how God – who's not the author of suffering – can still use it to shape our lives and refine our characters for his glory and the benefit of others.

In sharing the Gospel, we learn to expect the fact that events like the attack on the Twin Towers on September 11, 2001 in New York will be raised as an objection to the very existence of God. In responding to events like this, someone spoke for many when he said: 'I want to sue [God] for negligence, for being asleep at the wheel of the universe.' But we betray our instinctive morality when we react to things that happen by labelling them 'good' or 'evil'. Can words like 'good' or 'evil' really have meaning if we don't believe in God? One bold atheist, Oxford University's Richard Dawkins, would say 'no'. Since he doesn't believe in God, he also flatly says there's 'no evil and no good'. At least he's being consistent.

But suppose you were to accept there's no God – and so basically no 'good' or 'evil', can we then accept that September 11 is just a morally meaningless event in a meaningless world? If we feel we can't go that far, then we're forced to draw the conclusion that a consistent atheist doesn't appear to have any answers after all – and no basis for even asking the questions about the morality of such atrocities. The more you think about it, the more the existence of evil in our world points us towards the existence of God - and not away from it. Why? Because unless we refuse to label atrocities as 'evil', we're still faced with the reality of God. Suffering remains a tragic experience, the Christian perspective is not an easy one, but the atheist alternative is simply unrealistic.

Basically, what's the relevance of Christianity to the atrocities of this groaning world? Edward Shillito, while viewing the destruction of the Great War, helpfully wrote: 'to our wounds only God's wounds can speak'. Yes, there's pain and suffering at the heart of the Christian message, but it's not only human pain: it's the pain of God. After all we've said, a question mark remains over human suffering, but we do need to put it in the context of the cross of Christ – which is the mark of divine suffering. We may have to wait for justice and peace in the world, but we can know God's forgiveness for our sins on a personal level and be at peace with him right now. For God has joined us in suffering to give us the offer of ultimately being with him in a pain-free future: "He will wipe every tear from their eyes. There will be no more death or mourning or crying or pain, for the old order of things has passed away" (Revelation 21:4).

It's been said that suffering is not a question requiring an answer; nor is it a problem requiring a solution; but rather a mystery requiring a Presence. And that Presence is one which only the world-turning Christian Gospel can furnish for us.

FURTHER TITLES IN THIS SERIES

If you've enjoyed reading this book, first of all please consider taking a moment to leave a positive review on Amazon! Secondly, you may be interested to know that, at the date of the publishing of this book, the Search For Truth library now stands at almost fifty titles; each contains excellent reading material in a down-to-earth and conversational style, covering a wide range of topics from Bible character studies, theme studies, book studies, apologetics, prophecy, Christian living and more. The simplest way to access this material for purchase is by visiting Brian's Amazon author page:

Amazon.com: http://amzn.to/1u7rzIA

Amazon.co.uk: http://amzn.to/YZt5zC

Alternatively, the books can also be found simply by searching for the specific title or "Search For Truth Series" on Amazon. Paperback versions can also be purchased from Hayes Press at www.hayespress.org.

Take a look at some of the books in the library below:

PAPERBACK EDITIONS

The Supremacy of Christ

Nothing But Christ Crucified: First Corinthians

Christianity 101: 7 Bible Basics

Pure Milk: Nurturing the New Life in Jesus

Once Saved, Always Saved? The Reality of Eternal Salvation

Jesus: What Does the Bible Really Say?

The Tabernacle: God's House of Shadows

A Legacy of Kings: Israel's Chequered History

Healthy Churches: God's Bible Blueprint for Growth

Hope for Humanity: God's Fix for a Broken World

Fencepost Turtles: People Placed By God

Minor Prophets – Major Issues

Tribes and Tribulations – Israel's Predicted Personalities

Bible Answers to Listeners' Questions

One People for God Omnibus

Kings, Tribes and Prophets Omnibus

God – His Glory, His Building, His Son Omnibus

All these titles are also available in Kindle e-book format from Amazon.

EBOOK EDITIONS

Apologetics

Overcoming Objections to Christian Faith

Windows to Faith

Turning the World Upside Down

An Unchanging God?

Life, the Universe and Ultimate Answers

Bible Answers For Big Questions

Books of the Bible

Double Vision – The Insights of Isaiah

Unlocking Hebrews

James – The Epistle of Straw

The Visions of Zechariah

Experiencing God in Ephesians

Daniel Decoded

Bible Character Studies

Abraham – Friend of God

About The Bush – The Life of Moses

After God's Own Heart: The Life of David

Samson: A Type of Christ

Esther: A Date with Destiny

Discipleship

Praying with Paul

The Way: New Testament Discipleship

Power Outage: Christianity Unplugged

Closer Than a Brother – Christian Friendship

No Compromise!

Jesus Christ

Five Women and a Baby: The Genealogy of Jesus

They Met at the Cross – Five Encounters with Jesus

Salt and the Sacrifice of Christ

The Last Words of Jesus

Jesus: Son Over God's House

General Topics

The Kingdom of God – Past, Present or Future?

God's Appointment Calendar: The Feasts of Jehovah

Seeds – A Potted Bible History

AWOL! Bible Deserters and Defectors

5 Sacred Solos – The Truths That The Reformation
Recovered

Trees of the Bible

Knowing God: Reflections on Psalm 23

The Glory of God

Living in God's House

Answers to Listeners' Questions

Edge of Eternity – Approaching the End of Life

Tomorrow's Headlines – Bible Prophecy

The Five Loves of God

SEARCH FOR TRUTH RADIO BROADCASTS

Search for Truth Radio has been a ministry of the Churches of God (see www.churchesofgod.info) since 1978. Free Search for Truth podcasts can be listened to online or downloaded at four locations:

- At SFT's own dedicated podcast site: www.searchfortruth.podbean.com

- Via Itunes using the podcast app (search for 'Search For Truth')
- On the Churches of God website: (http://www.churchesofgod.info/search_for_truth_radi o_programmes.php)
- On the Transworld Radio website: (http://www.twr360.org/programs/ministry_id,103)

Alternatively, see below for details of digital and analogue radio timings.

Europe

Listen online at www.twr.org.uk/live.htm

SKY Digital Channel 0138 (11.390 GHz, ID 53555) and Freesat channel 790 and Freeview 733 in the **UK** - Saturday at 07.30 and Sunday at 06.45.

Malawi

Sunday on TWR Malawi FM Network at 06.45
UTC+2 (89.1 - 106.5 FM)

South East Asia

On Reach Beyond – Australia on Mondays 13.15
UTC, 25m band SW (15540 kHz.)

India

Tuesday and Friday on TWR Guam at 15.15, 19m
band SW (15110 kHz.)

Thailand

Wednesday on TWR Guam at 08.50, 19m band SW
(11965 kHz.)

Jamaica

Sunday on MegaJamz at 09.00, 98.7 FM

CONTACTING SEARCH FOR TRUTH

If you have enjoyed reading one of our books or listening to a radio broadcast, we would love to know about that, or answer any questions that you might have.

Contact us at:

SFT c/o Hayes, Press, The Barn, Flaxlands, Wootton Bassett, Swindon, Wiltshire SN4 8DY

P.O. Box 748, Ringwood, Victoria 3134, Australia

P.O. Box 70115, Chilomoni, Blantyre, Malawi

Web site: www.searchfortruth.org.uk

Email: sft@churchesofgod.info

Also, if you have enjoyed reading this book and/or others in the series, we would really appreciate it if you could just take a couple of minutes to leave a brief review on Amazon – it really is a very good way of spreading the word about our ministry – thanks and God bless!

Don't miss out!

Click the button below and you can sign up to receive emails whenever Brian Johnston publishes a new book. There's no charge and no obligation.

Sign Me Up!

https://books2read.com/r/B-A-VLMB-XJPK

BOOKS 2 READ

Connecting independent readers to independent writers.

Did you love *Nights of Old: Bible Stories of God at Work*?
Then you should read *First Corinthians: Nothing But Christ
Crucified* by Brian Johnston!

Bible teacher Brian Johnston unpacks the first letter of the
apostle Paul to the Corinthians in this informative book,
exploring such important topics as spiritual gifts, the body of
Christ, headcoverings, the Breaking of Bread and the powerful
wisdom of God in Christ crucified!